STORY
of
JESUS

STORY
of
JESUS

The Epic Account of His Life and Times on Earth

Edoardo Albert, Robin Griffith-Jones

FOX CHAPEL
PUBLISHING

©2023 by Future Publishing Limited

Articles in this issue are translated or reproduced from *Story of Jesus* and are the copyright of or licensed to Future Publishing Limited, a Future plc group company, UK 2022.

Used under license. All rights reserved. This version published by Fox Chapel Publishing Company, Inc., 903 Square Street, Mount Joy, PA 17552.

For more information about the Future plc group, go to **http://www.futureplc.com**.

ISBN 978-1-4971-0400-6

Library of Congress Cataloging-in-Publication Data

To learn more about the other great books from Fox Chapel Publishing, or to find a retailer near you, call toll-free 800-457-9112 or visit us at *www.FoxChapelPublishing.com*.

We are always looking for talented authors. To submit an idea, please send a brief inquiry to acquisitions@foxchapelpublishing.com.

Printed in China
First printing

Welcome to
STORY
of
JESUS

With over 2 billion followers alive today, Jesus Christ may be the most influential person to have ever walked the Earth.

The Story of Jesus relates the epic tale of Jesus' life, from the prophecies surrounding his birth and childhood in Nazareth, to his adult years spreading his ministry and gaining followers. Discover the people Jesus selected to be his Apostles, who would witness his most dramatic moments and carry forward his teachings. Uncover the truth behind Judas' betrayal, Jesus' encounter with Pilate, and the crucifixion at Golgotha. Packed with incredible imagery and insight into the period, this is the perfect guide for anyone who wants to unearth the true story of Jesus of Nazareth.

CONTENTS

76

106

122

54

Tumult in the Levant

Triumph and tragedy ebbed and flowed in the Levant prior to the coming of Jesus Christ and during his lifetime

BATTLE OF PANIUM

Panium near the Golan Heights † 200 BCE

Antiochus III, also known as Antiochus the Great, undertakes a campaign of conquest during the Fifth Syrian War. At the head of a Seleucid army, his forces engage an army under the Egyptian Ptolemaic General Scopus of Aetolia at Paneas, an ancient shrine to the god Pan near the source of the Jordan River. The Seleucid forces employ cataphracts, or armored cavalry, under the command of the Seleucid leader's son, Antiochus the Younger, and attack the flanks of the Ptolemaic forces. Driving the enemy cavalry before them, the cataphracts then turn to attack the Ptolemaic infantry from behind. The ensuing rout secures for Antiochus dominion over Palestine and Phoenicia, and the end of Ptolemaic rule in the Levant. Antiochus III grants substantial privilege to the Jewish population, and the formation of the Sanhedrin occurs within three years.

ANTIOCHUS IV PLUNDERS THE TEMPLE

Jerusalem † 169 BCE

Antiochus IV executes a sharp reversal of the freedoms the Jewish people have enjoyed under his father, Antiochus III. A systematic campaign of persecution and Hellenization of the Jews begins around 170 BCE, and while the king is consumed with a military campaign in Egypt, the deposed high priest Jason returns to Jerusalem and takes control of the city, deposing Menelaus, the high priest installed by Antiochus IV. When the king returns from Egypt, he assaults Jerusalem, plunders the Temple, and restores Menelaus, who favors continued Hellenization of the people. Antiochus IV subsequently outlaws the Jewish religion and all worship of the god Yahweh, and orders the worship of the Greek god Zeus as the supreme deity. Many Jews are slaughtered during this period of upheaval, and the city of Jerusalem is destroyed. Antiochus IV establishes a military fortress called the Acra.

| 230 BCE | 200 BCE | 192 BCE | 170 BCE | 169 BCE | 167 BCE | 166 BCE | 166 BCE |

ROME BEGINS EXPANSION INTO EASTERN MEDITERRANEAN

Central Mediterranean Basin † 230 BCE

ROMAN-SELEUCID WAR BEGINS

Central Mediterranean Asia Minor † 192 BCE

SELEUCID KING ANTIOCHUS IV INVADES EGYPT

Egypt † 170 BCE

BATTLE OF EMMAUS

Emmaus, West Of Jerusalem † 166 BCE

MACCABEAN REVOLT BEGINS

Judea † 167 BCE

The ruthless suspension of their freedoms, particularly to worship as they choose, sparks the traditional Jewish faction in Judea to rise against the rule of the Seleucids and those Jews who favor continuing Hellenization of their culture. Inevitably, the unrest precipitates open revolt under the leadership of Judah Maccabee, son of a traditional leader named Mattathias, who has slain a Hellenistic Jew and fled to the wilderness with his five sons. Judah embarks on a campaign of guerrilla warfare. During the period, the surname Maccabee, supposedly derived from the Aramaic word for 'hammer,' is bestowed on the fiery military leader.

BATTLE OF BETH HORON

Town of Beth Horon north of Jerusalem † 166 BCE

After soundly defeating a Seleucid army under the command of Apollonius, the rebel forces of Judah Maccabee confront another threat, a second Seleucid army commanded by Seron, governor of Syria. Exploiting Seron's overconfidence, Maccabee continues the effective tactic of ambush, and though Seron has tried to prepare for such an encounter, the speed and maneuverability of the Jewish fighters wins the day and costs Seron his life. The Seleucids cling to their slow, ponderous phalanx as a primary engine of battle, which costs them dearly. Within weeks, the stalwart Jewish rebels win another startling victory at the Battle of Emmaus.

FIRST HANNUKAH

Jerusalem † 164 BCE

With the success of the Jewish revolt led by Judah Maccabee against Seleucid control, the Second Temple in Jerusalem is reclaimed and rededicated, and Hannukah, derived from the Hebrew word meaning "to dedicate," is observed for the first time. Also known as the Feast of Lights, the season of Hannukah, beginning on the 25th day of Kislev according to the Jewish calendar, commemorates the day the Jews ceased fighting and the miracle of the olive oil that sustained a burning menorah for eight days although it appeared that enough oil was present for only a single day.

JONATHAN MACCABEE BECOMES JUDEAN RULER
Jerusalem † 152 BCE

THIRD PUNIC WAR ENDS
Carthage † 146 BCE

164 BCE	160 BCE	160 BCE	152 BCE	146BCE

JONATHAN MACCABEE ASSUMES LEADERSHIP JEWISH REVOLT
Emmaus, West Of Judea † 160 BCE

GREECE FALLS TO ROMAN RULE
Greece † 146 BCE

DEATH OF JUDAH MACCABEE

Elasa, Palestine near the modern city of Ramallah † 160 BCE

Despite the successes of the Jewish revolt against the Seleucids, the Acra remains in enemy hands. Meanwhile, Jewish communities are under attack by neighboring Hellenistic cities. Judah Maccabee and his followers remain at war, while an internal threat from Hellenized Jews emerges. The Seleucid King Demetrius I dispatches an army under Bacchides to Judea, forcing Maccabee to abandon Jerusalem and conduct a familiar guerrilla campaign until Bacchides withdraws to Antioch. Maccabee returns to Jerusalem, only to be threatened by another Seleucid army under Nicanor, which his forces destroy at Adasa. When he learns of Nacanor's defeat, Demetrius I again sends Bacchides to Judea with an army of 20,000 troops. At the Battle of Elasa, many of Maccabee's fighters withdraw in the face of overwhelming numerical superiority. However, Judah and small force stand their ground, and he is killed in battle.

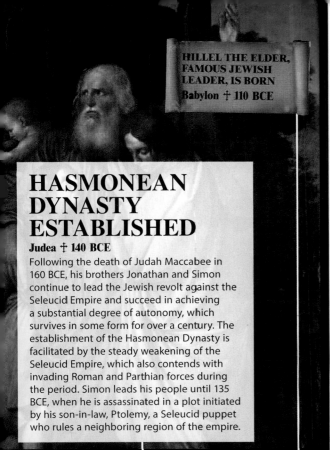

HASMONEAN DYNASTY ESTABLISHED

Judea † 140 BCE

Following the death of Judah Maccabee in 160 BCE, his brothers Jonathan and Simon continue to lead the Jewish revolt against the Seleucid Empire and succeed in achieving a substantial degree of autonomy, which survives in some form for over a century. The establishment of the Hasmonean Dynasty is facilitated by the steady weakening of the Seleucid Empire, which also contends with invading Roman and Parthian forces during the period. Simon leads his people until 135 BCE, when he is assassinated in a plot initiated by his son-in-law, Ptolemy, a Seleucid puppet who rules a neighboring region of the empire.

HASMONEAN CIVIL WAR BEGINS

Judea † 67 BCE

The Hasmonean Dynasty exists as a regional semiautonomous kingdom within the Seleucid Empire and reaches the zenith of its influence and power during the reigns of King Alexander Jannaeus and Queen Salome Alexandra, who rule from about 103 to 67 BCE, as Salome survives her husband for a decade. After the death of Salome, a simmering rivalry between their two sons, Aristobulus and Hyrcanus, erupts in civil war. Each is supported by the Sadducees and Pharisees respectively, opposing factions within the Jewish community, while Aristobulus hires mercenary troops and Hyrcanus receives support from the Nabataean Kingdom of Arabia. Hyrcanus has reigned as king only briefly when his brother rises against him, and the civil war proves disastrous for the Jews. Aristobulus gains the upper hand and forces Hyrcanus to flee to sanctuary with the Nabataeans after abdicating the throne. Both brothers solicit the intervention of the Roman Empire, attempting to bribe Marcus Aemilius Scaurus, an influential political figure in Syria. Scaurus supports Aristobulus, who temporarily prevails.

142BCE	140 BCE	134 BCE	110 BCE	71 BCE	69 BCE	67 BCE	63 BCE

JEWISH
ISOLATIONISTS
OCCUPY QUMRAN
SETTLEMENT
Qumran, Judea † 134
BCE

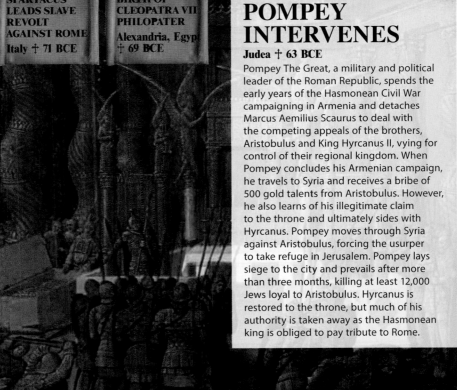

POMPEY INTERVENES

Judea † 63 BCE

Pompey The Great, a military and political leader of the Roman Republic, spends the early years of the Hasmonean Civil War campaigning in Armenia and detaches Marcus Aemilius Scaurus to deal with the competing appeals of the brothers, Aristobulus and King Hyrcanus II, vying for control of their regional kingdom. When Pompey concludes his Armenian campaign, he travels to Syria and receives a bribe of 500 gold talents from Aristobulus. However, he also learns of his illegitimate claim to the throne and ultimately sides with Hyrcanus. Pompey moves through Syria against Aristobulus, forcing the usurper to take refuge in Jerusalem. Pompey lays siege to the city and prevails after more than three months, killing at least 12,000 Jews loyal to Aristobulus. Hyrcanus is restored to the throne, but much of his authority is taken away as the Hasmonean king is obliged to pay tribute to Rome.

CANONIZATION OF THE HEBREW BIBLE

Judea † 140 BCE

The canonization of the Hebrew Bible begins, although modern scholars have yet to achieve consensus on the accuracy of this date, which falls during the Hasmonean Dynasty. According to some scholars the process is completed about a century later around 40 BCE. The Hebrew Bible's 24 books are commonly referred to as the Tanakh, which is divided into three sections, Torah, Prophets, and Writings, not strictly on content but due to the fact that the groups were concluded at separate times over a lengthy period. The earliest canonization is that of the Torah, which occurs sometime prior to 400 BCE.

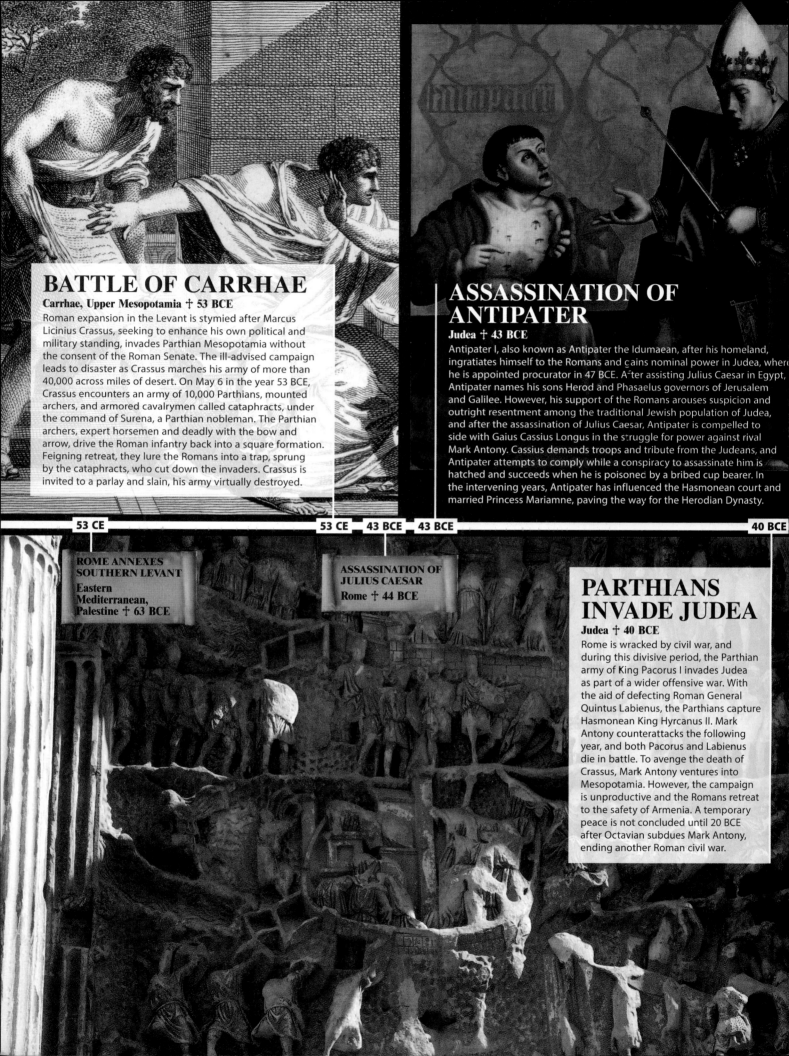

BATTLE OF CARRHAE

Carrhae, Upper Mesopotamia † 53 BCE

Roman expansion in the Levant is stymied after Marcus Licinius Crassus, seeking to enhance his own political and military standing, invades Parthian Mesopotamia without the consent of the Roman Senate. The ill-advised campaign leads to disaster as Crassus marches his army of more than 40,000 across miles of desert. On May 6 in the year 53 BCE, Crassus encounters an army of 10,000 Parthians, mounted archers, and armored cavalrymen called cataphracts, under the command of Surena, a Parthian nobleman. The Parthian archers, expert horsemen and deadly with the bow and arrow, drive the Roman infantry back into a square formation. Feigning retreat, they lure the Romans into a trap, sprung by the cataphracts, who cut down the invaders. Crassus is invited to a parlay and slain, his army virtually destroyed.

ASSASSINATION OF ANTIPATER

Judea † 43 BCE

Antipater I, also known as Antipater the Idumaean, after his homeland, ingratiates himself to the Romans and gains nominal power in Judea, where he is appointed procurator in 47 BCE. After assisting Julius Caesar in Egypt, Antipater names his sons Herod and Phasaelus governors of Jerusalem and Galilee. However, his support of the Romans arouses suspicion and outright resentment among the traditional Jewish population of Judea, and after the assassination of Julius Caesar, Antipater is compelled to side with Gaius Cassius Longus in the struggle for power against rival Mark Antony. Cassius demands troops and tribute from the Judeans, and Antipater attempts to comply while a conspiracy to assassinate him is hatched and succeeds when he is poisoned by a bribed cup bearer. In the intervening years, Antipater has influenced the Hasmonean court and married Princess Mariamne, paving the way for the Herodian Dynasty.

53 CE — **53 CE** — **43 BCE** — **43 BCE** — **40 BCE**

ROME ANNEXES SOUTHERN LEVANT

Eastern Mediterranean, Palestine † 63 BCE

ASSASSINATION OF JULIUS CAESAR

Rome † 44 BCE

PARTHIANS INVADE JUDEA

Judea † 40 BCE

Rome is wracked by civil war, and during this divisive period, the Parthian army of King Pacorus I invades Judea as part of a wider offensive war. With the aid of defecting Roman General Quintus Labienus, the Parthians capture Hasmonean King Hyrcanus II. Mark Antony counterattacks the following year, and both Pacorus and Labienus die in battle. To avenge the death of Crassus, Mark Antony ventures into Mesopotamia. However, the campaign is unproductive and the Romans retreat to the safety of Armenia. A temporary peace is not concluded until 20 BCE after Octavian subdues Mark Antony, ending another Roman civil war.

HEROD BECOMES KING

Judea † 37 BCE

Herod the Great, son of Antipater the Idumaean, rises to the throne of Judea as a Roman vassal king after overthrowing Antigonus, the last Hasmonean King of Judea in a three-year war. Herod reigns for approximately 40 years until sometime between 4 BCE and 1 CE, embarking on an ambitious building program that includes the construction of the Temple Mount in Jerusalem. At the same time, he ruthlessly extinguishes threats from the dislodged Hasmoneans and others to gain the throne. Herod is remembered for his suppression of his Jewish subjects and as the Biblical ruler of Judea during the time of the birth of Jesus Christ. He is vilified in Biblical texts as the instigator of the Massacre of the Innocents, ordering the deaths of all male children under two years of age after being told by the Magi that they are seeking the one who is "born King of the Jews." Herod's sons inherit his crown, perpetuating the Herodian Dynasty.

OCAVIAN TRIUMPHS IN BATTLE OF ACTIUM

Actium, Ionian Sea † 31 BCE

OCTAVIAN BECOMES AUGUSTUS

Rome † 27 BCE

Octavian, great nephew and adopted son of Julius Caesar, becomes Emperor of Rome, changing his name to Augustus four years after the defeat of his rival, Mark Antony, in the Battle of Actium. Ruling for 40 years until 14 CE, Augustus initiates two centuries known as the Pax Romana; the empire is free from large-scale conflicts, although territorial wars and the suppression of uprisings continue. Augustus is emperor of Rome during the time of the birth of Jesus Christ, extending the taxation decree that brings Joseph and Mary to Bethlehem.

| 37 BCE | 31 BCE | 27 BCE | 20 BCE |

HEROD EXTENDS TEMPLE MOUNT

Jerusalem † 20 BCE

Well known for his lavish spending on numerous construction projects, Herod the Great begins construction of an extension of the Temple Mount in Jerusalem, a portion of which stands to this day and is known as the Western Wall. Three Islamic structures, the Dome of the Rock, Dome of the Chains, and al-Aqsa Mosque now stand on the site as well. Herod extends the natural plateau of a mountain overlooking the Kidron Valley with four immense retaining walls and the transport of fill material to level the surface. He also begins an extensive expansion of the Second Temple in the hope of gaining favor with the Jewish people and constructing a city that has few rivals in its grandeur. The First Temple had been built by King Solomon and the second by Zerubbabel. Hebrew tradition relates that the Third Temple will be erected on the site as well.

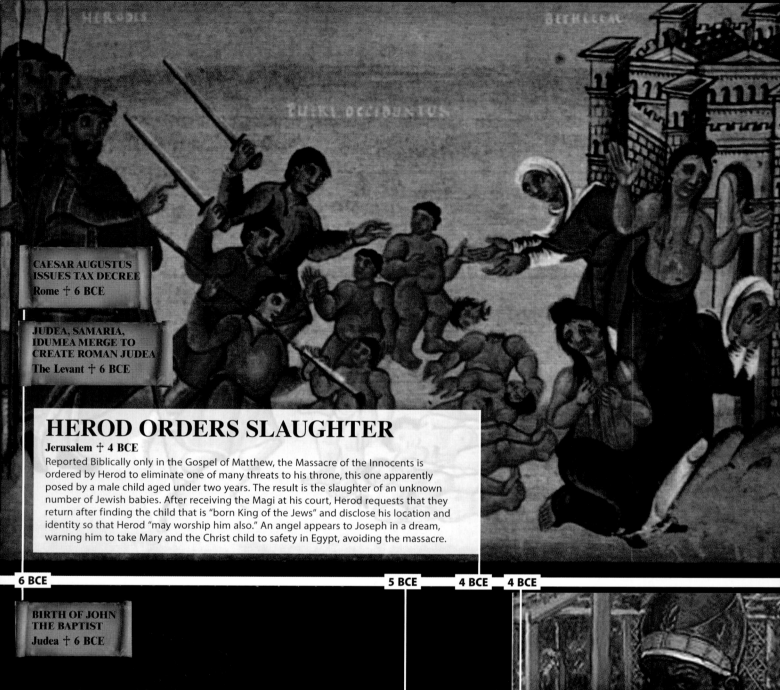

CAESAR AUGUSTUS
ISSUES TAX DECREE
Rome ✝ 6 BCE

JUDEA, SAMARIA,
IDUMEA MERGE TO
CREATE ROMAN JUDEA
The Levant ✝ 6 BCE

HEROD ORDERS SLAUGHTER

Jerusalem ✝ 4 BCE

Reported Biblically only in the Gospel of Matthew, the Massacre of the Innocents is ordered by Herod to eliminate one of many threats to his throne, this one apparently posed by a male child aged under two years. The result is the slaughter of an unknown number of Jewish babies. After receiving the Magi at his court, Herod requests that they return after finding the child that is "born King of the Jews" and disclose his location and identity so that Herod "may worship him also." An angel appears to Joseph in a dream, warning him to take Mary and the Christ child to safety in Egypt, avoiding the massacre.

6 BCE   **5 BCE**   **4 BCE**   **4 BCE**

BIRTH OF JOHN
THE BAPTIST
Judea ✝ 6 BCE

HEROD'S KINGDOM DIVIDED

Jerusalem ✝ 4 BCE

Although the exact date of Herod The Great's death is unknown, his sons inherit his former kingdom around 4 BCE. Although they remain vassals of the Roman Empire, the sons each receive a portion of their father's former domain. Herod Archelaus receives Judea, Sumeria, and Edom and rules for a decade until approximately 6 CE, when he is banished to Gaul. A second son, Herod Philip I, receives a region in the northeast and remains in nominal control until his own death in 34 CE. The third son, Herod Antipas, becomes ruler of Galilee and Perea until his exile to Gaul by order of Roman Emperor Caligula in 39 CE. Herod Antipas is believed to be the ruler referenced Biblically during the murder of John The Baptist and the trial and crucifixion of Jesus. Agrippa I, grandson of Herod The Great and a friend of Caligula, is given control of territories formerly belonging to Herod Philip I and Herod Antipas. His son, Agrippa II, is the last king of the Herodian Dynasty.

BIRTH OF JESUS

Bethlehem, Judea ✝ 5 BCE

Although the exact year of the birth of Jesus of Nazareth is unknown, scholars assert that it occurs sometime between 11 BCE and 4 BCE, probably during the month of September, since there are Biblical references to shepherds tending sheep outdoors through the night and the livestock would be housed indoors during cold winter temperatures. The weather that time of year also remains favorable for long travel, such as undertaken by Joseph and Mary. The Gospel of Luke cites the period during which Quirinius, governor of Syria, mandates a census, and this event is known to occur in 6 CE.

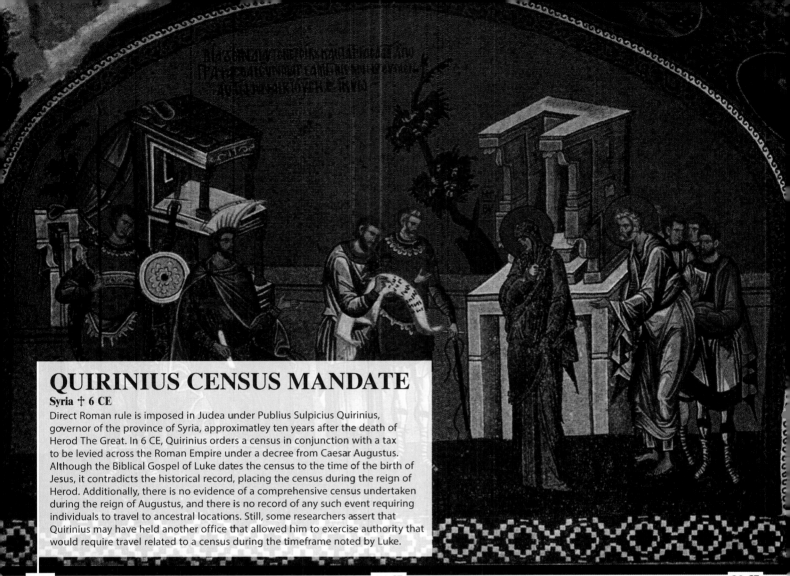

QUIRINIUS CENSUS MANDATE

Syria † 6 CE

Direct Roman rule is imposed in Judea under Publius Sulpicius Quirinius, governor of the province of Syria, approximatley ten years after the death of Herod The Great. In 6 CE, Quirinius orders a census in conjunction with a tax to be levied across the Roman Empire under a decree from Caesar Augustus. Although the Biblical Gospel of Luke dates the census to the time of the birth of Jesus, it contradicts the historical record, placing the census during the reign of Herod. Additionally, there is no evidence of a comprehensive census undertaken during the reign of Augustus, and there is no record of any such event requiring individuals to travel to ancestral locations. Still, some researchers assert that Quirinius may have held another office that allowed him to exercise authority that would require travel related to a census during the timeframe noted by Luke.

PONTIUS PILATE APPOINTED

Jerusalem † 26 CE

Appointed during the reign of Emperor Tiberius, Pontius Pilate becomes the fifth prefect of the Roman province of Judea. The extension of Roman rule in the eastern region, Pilate is identified as the official who allows an enflamed mob of Jewish citizens to condemn Jesus to death during the religious observance of Passover. Although Pilate offers that he finds no criminal guilt in Jesus, he nevertheless acquiesces to the crowd and hands the messianic teacher over for crucifixion, symbolically washing his hands of the situation and hoping to maintain order in the streets of Jerusalem. Herod Antipas, puppet ruler of Galilee, also pronounces that he finds Jesus guilty of no crime. Pilate is later removed from office after brutally suppressing an uprising in Samaria. Returning to Rome, he dies around 36 CE.

CRUCIFIXION OF JESUS

Jerusalem † 30 CE

Arrested in the Garden of Gethsemane, Jesus is accused of blasphemy and treason at a trial before the Sanhedrin, the Jewish tribunal in Jerusalem. He is then transferred to Pontius Pilate for pronouncement of sentence, and though Pilate finds Jesus guilty of no crime, the Sanhedrin clamor for his execution due to unrest and questioning of the status quo he has caused. According to Biblical accounts, Jesus is beaten and made to wear a crown of thorns as Roman soldiers mock him, and crowds line the street as he carries his cross to the hill of Golgotha, the Place of the Skull, where he is crucified with two thieves. The Gospel of Mark states the execution begins around 9 a.m., and that at 3 p.m. Jesus dies. The exact year of the crucifixion is believed to be somtime between 30 CE and 33 CE.

Levant and Legacy

Judea and Galilee, ancient lands of the Hebrew people, were governed by great powers and hotbeds of political and religious tumult in the time of Jesus

WRITTEN BY MICHAEL HASKEW

In 323 BCE, Alexander the Great, the legendary Macedonian-born conqueror of the known world, died before he could consolidate his empire. Subsequently, his generals carved vast territories for themselves from Alexander's land. As masters of the Levant, they followed the Assyrians, Babylonians, and Persians, each influencing the culture of the ancient Hebrew people.

Generals Ptolemy and Seleucus Nicator secured Egypt, and Asia Minor and the Middle East respectively; however, they became rivals and fought for control of the Levant, an area stretching from the Mediterranean Sea east to Mesopotamia, and from the Sinai Desert in the south to the Taurus Mountains in the north. At the decisive Battle of Panium in 200 BCE, the Seleucid (or Syrian-Greek) army extinguished Ptolemaic (or Egyptian-Greek) supremacy in the region.

Greek (Hellenistic) influence on culture remained pervasive in the eastern Mediterranean and the Middle East, including the land of ancient Israel, primarily Galilee in the north and Judea in the south. Alexander's heirs founded cities and colonies that flourished economically. Simultaneously, the Hellenistic philosophical, theological, and social perspective on the world was propagated. A pantheon of gods, a flowering of literature, art, and mathematics, and advances in architecture and science were accompanied by a lifestyle that by strict Hebrew standards was decadent.

For 150 years, the Seleucids controlled a sprawling empire that included the Levant. On the fringes of the empire, however, the Hellenistic hold on society either began to fray or had never captured the popular spirit. The interior of the Levant was particularly insulated as deserts and other natural barriers made population centers distant. Small settlements, nomadic tribesmen, and traditional Hebrew peoples were largely untouched by the wave of Hellenistic thought and practice that shaped much of the Western world.

Faith of the Fathers

The oldest sector of Jerusalem, known as the City of David, was a small concentration of life in the Levant, particularly in comparison to the thriving metropolises of the Mediterranean coast. While many Jews embraced Hellenization and at least partially assimilated into Greek life, there remained a stalwart group of Jews that defended traditional faith, the worship of a single god, Yahweh, and the observance of laws as recorded in the early writings of Jewish religious leaders. Despite its diminutive stature, Jerusalem and the territories of Judea and Galilee remained largely resistant to Hellenization.

The traditional Jews recoiled at the 'excesses' of Greek society. Hellenes engaged in behavior that, according to Jewish law, was at times punishable by death. Those Jews corrupted by Greek influence were apostate, Jews in name only. Conversely, the high priests appealed to

The Levant plays host to many important people and events in the three Abrahamic religions

François-Joseph Heim's Study for Destruction of Jerusalem by the Romans is filled with dramatic action

the nomadic herdsmen and pilgrims who made the journey to Jerusalem for religious observances and festivals.

Although relations between the hardline Jews and the Seleucids were cooperative at first, the death of King Antiochus III brought an abrupt end to peaceful coexistence. By 170 BCE, Antiochus IV initiated a systematic persecution of those Jews who resisted Hellenization. The

while employing guerrilla tactics against the armies sent to suppress the uprising. The surname "Maccabee" is derived from the Aramaic word meaning "hammer." The revolt continued after Judah's death at the Battle of Elasa in 160. His brothers, Jonathan and Simon, became its leaders, and Simon is credited with establishing the Hasmonean dynasty, the first semi-autonomous rule of the Jewish people in more than 400 years.

desecrating it. From this moment forward, the Hasmonean rulers of Judea were held under Roman authority.

The security of the frontier of the Roman Empire and the questionable loyalty of many Jewish people who refused to accept foreign rule remained problematic as puppet kings and city-states were established under indirect Roman supervision. In Judea, Herod the Great succeeded with his Roman benefactors in securing the throne against Parthian enemies. In 37 BCE, Herod was proclaimed King of Judea, while traditional Jewish antipathy simmered below the surface for at least 30 years and among the people, the concept of the 'Messiah'—a deliverer that would free them from oppression—became a popular theme. The idea gained further support following the death of Herod in 4 BCE, the imposition of direct Roman rule, and the annexation of much of the Levant into the Roman province of Judea.

"In 37 BCE, Herod was proclaimed King of Judea, while traditional Jewish antipathy simmered below the surface"

resulting unrest erupted in open rebellion as traditional Jewish followers fought the Seleucids for independence. The defining moment came around 167 BCE when Mattathias ben Johanan, from a family of rural priests in the town of Modi'in, was asked by the Seleucid representative in his hometown to perform a sacrifice to the Greek gods. Mattathias refused and in his righteous anger killed a Hellenized Jew who had stepped forward to comply. He also killed the Seleucid official who requested the sacrifice.

Judah the Hammer

Mattathias fled to the countryside with his five sons, and soon a widespread revolt threatened the mastery of the Seleucids. Judah Maccabee, one of the sons, became leader of the insurrection, winning victories

By then, the traditional Jewish faith had matured under foreign rule, solidifying doctrine with the traditionalists seeking the return of the Jewish monarchy of old, ruled from Jerusalem and encompassing territories once under control of King David and his son, King Solomon. Hebrew remained as a literary and legal written language, but the day-to-day language of the people became Aramaic. Nevertheless, the Hasmonean dynasty was plagued by civil war. Infighting and external threats from surrounding powers led to an appeal to Rome to intervene in the continuing unrest. Pompey the Great, campaigning in Armenia, dispatched a subordinate to deal with rival brothers, each claiming the throne. In 63 BCE, Pompey personally brought an army to Jerusalem, laid siege, and took the city. He even entered the Holy of Holies, thereby

The Birth of Jesus

Amid Roman hegemony and the polarization of the Jewish people from those who accepted assimilation into the Roman way of

This artist's rendering depicts Solomon's reconstruction of the Temple in Jerusalem based on information from Bible texts

"By 170 BCE, Antiochus IV initiated a systematic persecution of those Jews who resisted Hellenization"

In this 14th century illustration, Roman forces breach the walls of Jerusalem and destroy the Temple during the Great Revolt

Jewish Revolts Against Rome

In time, the Jewish people rebelled forcefully against Roman rule. The first revolt, known to history as the Great Revolt, occurred from 66-73 CE, about 30 years after the crucifixion of Jesus. The imposition of taxes by the Romans incited the unrest, adding to an oppressive rule in Judea that had continually intensified for years. In response, the Zealots, a faction of militant Jews that sanctioned whatever means possible to end Roman rule, emerged. The Jews further refused to deify Emperor Caligula (Gaius Caesar), and when the last Roman procurator, Flavius, confiscated a large cache of silver from the Temple in Jerusalem in 66 CE, violence erupted.

Following an inconclusive victory over the small Roman garrison in Jerusalem, the rebels were confronted with an overwhelming force of at least 60,000 well-trained Roman soldiers. The rebellion was ruthlessly crushed by the Roman forces, particularly in northern Galilee, a hotbed of unrest. As many as a million Jews were killed in the conflict, and in 70 CE the Romans sacked Jerusalem and destroyed the Temple. Sixty years later, the Bar Kokhba revolt was also suppressed. These revolts were the most calamitous events in Jewish history prior to the Holocaust. Two millennia of exile and the absence of a Jewish political voice in Israel persisted until the founding of the modern Jewish state in 1948. ∎

life and those that steadfastly refused to bow to the authority of Caesar, the birth of Jesus was quite probably an event that went largely unnoticed. Biblical accounts of an angelic host and the Magi that journeyed to visit the child are harbingers of the tremendous influence the adult Jesus would exert during a brief ministry on Earth that is believed to have lasted no more than three years.

According to the Gospel of Luke, it was customary for the Jews to congregate in Jerusalem for the observance of the Passover celebration. When Jesus was just 12 years old, he was separated from his parents, Mary and Joseph, who believed he was with them but traveling homeward in company with friends and relatives. After traveling for a day, the parents were unable to locate their son. They quickly returned to Jerusalem and searched for three days before finding him among the rabbis in the Temple. Mary naturally expressed her concern, but young Jesus replied that the parents should have known that he could be found in his "Father's house."

Luke relates that Mary paused to consider the implications of her son's wisdom, which

had astonished the Temple elders, and Jesus grew in both "wisdom and in stature and in favor with God and man." From that time, virtually nothing is known of the life of Jesus until the beginning of his ministry approximately 18 years later. The accounts of the Gospels of Matthew, Mark, Luke, and John, however, are apparently not intended as standard biographical texts. Rather, they are allegorical in nature, written to encourage a deepening faith in the Messiah, brought to Earth by God through immaculate conception, born to a virgin and a carpenter, the true Son of the Most High, whose mission was to atone for the sins of mankind and reconcile them with their Creator.

Mission and Fulfillment

At about the age of 30, Jesus is believed to have undertaken his Earthly ministry. While John the Baptist is preaching in the wilderness, Jesus comes to the banks of the River Jordan near Bethabara, where he is baptized by John. Born in Judea and reared in Galilee in the town of Nazareth, Jesus walks into the Judean desert and faces the temptations of the devil before beginning an

itinerant ministry. He preaches at Capernaum on the northern shore of the Sea of Galilee, and the town becomes a center of activity for Jesus as he calls the first five of his 12 disciples, including the fisherman brothers, Peter and Andrew, and Philip, all three of whom hailed from the village of Bethsaida.

At a wedding in Cana of Galilee, Jesus turns water into wine, his first recorded miracle. His travels take him to Jerusalem in Judea, likely for the observance of Passover, and then into Samaria, where he encounters the Samaritan woman at the well in the village of Sychar. While in Cana, he heals the son of a royal official who lies near death in Capernaum. Jesus preaches in his hometown of Nazareth, and the people reject him, threatening to throw him from a cliff.

Jesus reportedly heals many people. At Capernaum, he restores a raving madman in the synagogue and dispels a fever from Peter's own mother-in-law. Returning to Jerusalem, he heals a crippled man at the Pool of Bethesda. Walking again to Capernaum, he heals the daughter of a Roman centurion's servant and soon calms the stormy Sea of Galilee as the disciples

© Alamy

Following his arrest, Jesus stands trial before the Sanhedrin in Jerusalem. He is subsequently brought to Roman procurator Pontius Pilate

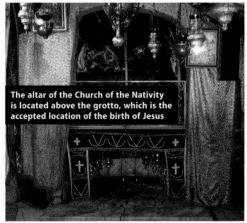

The altar of the Church of the Nativity is located above the grotto, which is the accepted location of the birth of Jesus

Jesus greets his prospective disciples at the Sea of Galilee during their miraculous catch of fish after following his directive

A classic example of Seleucid artwork is this statue of a prince from the 2nd or 3rd century BCE

huddle aboard a small boat in the midst of the gale. On the northwestern shore, probably near the village of Tabgha, he delivers the Sermon on the Mount. At Bethsaida, he performs the miracle of the loaves and fishes, feeding a throng of 5,000 with only the food a small boy has brought to the gathering. The disciples board a boat to return across the Sea of Galilee, and Jesus walks on the water to meet them.

Jesus then ventures into Phoenicia and visits the area of Sidon and Tyre along the eastern coast of the Mediterranean Sea. Traveling through Galilee, he continues healing in the region of the Decapolis and miraculously feeds 4,000 people who have followed him for three days. In the northern province of Gaulanitis at the town of Caesarea Philippi, Jesus asks his disciples, "Who do you say I am?" Peter replies that Jesus is the Messiah. Jesus travels to Mount Tabor in southern Galilee and ascends the peak with Peter, James, and John. The Transfiguration occurs as Jesus becomes radiant with heavenly light and converses with the spirits of Moses and Elijah. He moves through Perea on the east bank of the River Jordan and then to Jericho, just north of the Dead Sea, where he converts Zaccheus the tax collector. Along the way he also encounters a blind man and restores his sight. In Samaria, he famously heals the ten lepers, and at Bethany he raises Lazarus from the dead.

At last, for six days Jesus remains in the house of Lazarus, Mary, and Martha, and travels into Jerusalem, returning in the evening. On the Sunday before Passover, commemorated by Christians as Palm Sunday, he fulfils prophecy by riding into Jerusalem on a donkey amid a jubilant crowd. During the last week of his life, he ejects money changers from the Temple, conducts a ritual last meal with his disciples, is betrayed in the Garden of Gethsemane by Judas, and comes before the ruling priests of the Sanhedrin, jealous of his popularity and threatened by his message of a restoration of God's kingdom—not to mention the widespread rumor that he is the Messiah.

Tried before the Sanhedrin and brought before Pontius Pilate, the Roman prefect, Jesus is ultimately sentenced to death by crucifixion after being publicly flogged and mocked by a crowd. Biblical texts relate that the execution took place on a Friday and the agony lasted for six hours until 3 p.m., when his death was marked by an earthquake and the tearing of the Temple veil, signifying the atonement for sin and opening the way for all into the Holy of Holies. The Bible further records that Jesus rose from the dead on the third day and made several appearances to the faithful before his ascension into heaven.

Although the life of Jesus was short, only 32 or 33 years, his impact on religion, culture, philosophy, and human history is undeniable.

Judaea Province in the 1st Century

Phoenicia

Damascus

Tyre

Caesarea Philippi

Caesarea Philippi
Near Ceasarea Philippi, Peter confesses that Jesus is the Messiah in response to the question, "Who do you say that I am?" Jesus also heals a woman from Paneas who had been afflicted with bleeding for 12 years. The ruins of the palace of Agrippa and the temple of Pan are located there.

Ptolemais

Bethsaida

Nazareth
Bible texts indicate that Jesus grew up in the town of Nazareth in southern Galilee, with 17 New Testament references to "Jesus of Nazareth." Although the town was quite small, archaeological evidence of Roman habitation has been discovered, and religious shrines have been erected at numerous sites relating to the life of Jesus.

Tiberias

Sepphoris

Nazareth

Hippos

Bethsaida
Jesus heals a blind man outside Bethsaida on the northern shore of the Sea of Galilee. He also called Peter, Andrew, and Philip, who hailed from the town, to be his early disciples. The name of the town means "House of Hunting or Fishing" in Hebrew, and ruins of the ancient fishing village remain.

Mediterranean Sea

Caesarea

Bethabara

Scythopolis

Pella

Galilee

Decapolis

Sea of Galilee
This large lake is a focal point of Jesus' ministry in the New Testament. He crosses it by boat, delivers the Sermon on the Mount near its shores, calms a storm that sweeps over it, and walks on water to meet his disciples. Ruins of ancient villages have been discovered along its shores.

Samaria

maria

Sychar

Shechem

Bethabara
The ruins of Al-Maghtas, meaning "baptism" or "immersion" in Arabic, mark the place where Jesus came to John the Baptist and was baptized in the waters of the River Jordan prior to beginning his ministry. A mound known as Elijah's Hill and the remnants of a monastery are preserved.

Joppa

River Jordan

Philadelphia

Emmaus
Biblical texts relate that after his resurrection, Jesus meets two travelers on the road to Emmaus, discusses the events that have recently transpired and the prophecy of Moses, and shares a meal before disappearing as they finally recognize who he is. Discoveries of Jewish artifacts and settlement in the village have occurred.

ydda

Ephraim

Jericho

Emmaus

Qumaran

Jerusalem

Bethlehem

Judea

Bethlehem
In the fulfilment of prophecy, Jesus is born in Bethlehem, probably sometime from 11 BCE to 4 BCE. His parents, Joseph and Mary, had gone to the ancient City of David during a Roman-decreed census. The Church of the Nativity is constructed atop the grotto, a cave believed to be the location of the birth.

Machaerus

Nabatea

Dead Sea

Gaza

Jerusalem
Jesus visits Jerusalem more than once in his lifetime. His triumphal entry on Palm Sunday initiates the end of his Earthly ministry. He is tried and executed on the hill of Golgotha, the place of the skull. Ruins of the western wall of the Temple and numerous other religious shrines are found in the city.

Masaba

The Jewish Jesus in a Roman World

What was life like for the Jewish people of the Roman empire at the time of Jesus?

WRITTEN BY JON WRIGHT

Rome often pursued a broadly tolerant approach to the diverse religious traditions spread across its vast territories. Provided a faith was not perceived as a morally corrosive threat, and so long as it did not provoke rebellion or strife, it was permitted. Such a policy shouldn't necessarily be seen as a precursor to modern ideas of unfettered religious freedom. It was a matter of pragmatism; a useful way to accommodate the needs of so many religious groups and limit levels of resentment at Roman intrusion. Nonetheless, it was a welcome dispensation and one to which the Jewish people had full access by the time of Jesus. Both Julius Caesar and the emperor Augustus had issued formal edicts to protect Jewish rights. In 1 BCE, for example, Augustus declared that "the Jews shall use their own customs in accordance with their ancestral law . . . their sacred offerings shall be inviolable . . . [and] if anyone is detected stealing their sacred books or their sacred monies . . . he shall be considered sacrilegious."

Jews were entitled to practice their religion unhindered and celebrate all their festivals. They were exempt from military service—largely because their dietary rules and Sabbath observance made their involvement in the army impractical. They were exempt from attending court on the Sabbath and were not required to make sacrifices to the emperor as a deity, since this would have

flown in the face of their monotheistic beliefs. It was expected, however, that daily sacrifices should be made at the Jerusalem Temple for the empire and the emperor as a civic leader, though this was construed as more an act of homage than devotion. The Roman authorities were also alert to Jewish sensibilities concerning images of men and animals—outlawed on a strict reading of the commandment against graven images. Jews in Jerusalem were not required to include pictures of the emperor on the coins they minted and, for the most part, when Roman troops came into the city they did not carry their usual image-festooned banners.

The system was hardly perfect, as indicated by numerous complaints about such rules and protections being flouted, and throughout the 1st century, Jews in various parts of the empire would suffer harassment, banishments, and worse. Still, the empire often sought to facilitate the traditional patterns of Jewish life, insisting, for example, that the annual Temple tax, which Jews throughout the diaspora sent straight to Jerusalem, should not be interfered with.

The key organizations of Jewish culture were also respected by the Romans. In legal matters, for instance, cases between Jews could be adjudicated according to Jewish law. In Jerusalem, the pinnacle of the Jewish legal system, the Great Sanhedrin, enjoyed autonomy, even though it technically

This relief depicts Romans carrying away the Menorah from the Temple at Jerusalem during the Jewish revolt

Life in the Jewish Diaspora

The Jewish community in and around Jesus' homeland was, in many ways, markedly different from contemporary Jewish culture in other areas of the diaspora. Precise figures are hard to determine, but perhaps seven-eighths of 1st-century Jews lived within the boundaries of the Roman Empire: from Egypt and Asia Minor, to Crete, North Africa, and Eastern Europe. In many places, Jews only represented a small fraction of the population and this encouraged the establishment of Jewish enclaves—very different from the pervasive Jewish presence in Palestine.

Rome had somewhere between 20,000 and 60,000 Jews during this period, probably closer to the lower estimate. Numbers had been greatly boosted in the wake of Roman invasions of the Middle East in the 1st century BCE, which brought many Jews to the capital. They arrived as slaves, but the Jewish community often took rapid action to ransom them to freedom. Jews in Rome were painfully aware of how suddenly and violently fortunes could change: they had been expelled in 139 BCE and similar assaults would recur during the 1st century. In 19 CE the emperor Tiberius forced 4,000 Jewish men into military service (overturning traditional exemptions) and expelled all other Jews from Rome. Jews in such diaspora cities faced a tension between the needs of assimilation (which was routinely accomplished at a linguistic level and in terms of individuals taking up some positions in public life) and the imperative of sustaining ancient traditions. The latter cause was greatly helped by the devotion to Jerusalem which permeated every area of the Jewish diaspora. ∎

The emperor Tiberius, who expelled the Jews from the city of Rome

A reconstruction of how the Second Temple in Jerusalem may have appeared

required Roman permission to meet. Its 71 sages, headed by the Nasi, assembled every day except the Sabbath and festivals, and dealt with everything from ritual disputes to adultery, and from regulating the Jewish calendar to tithes. Lesser sanhedrins were also to be found in towns across the Middle East.

The Political Backdrop

Judaism, in sum, was what the Romans referred to as a *religio licita*—a fully legal and recognized faith. This provided, at least in theory, some measure of security, especially in a place such as Palestine, where the Jewish population was in a clear majority. The degree to which practice matched the theory still depended on contingent political factors. However, expansive the degree of toleration, the Jews of the Middle East could hardly ignore that they were under Roman rule. Pompey the Great's conquest of the Syrian province in 64 BCE, and the capture of Jerusalem in the following year, had been, according to the Jewish historian Flavius Josephus, "a disaster . . . we lost our liberty and became subjects to the Romans." The memory of Pompey striding into the Temple's Holy of Holies, where non-Jews were never

allowed, would scar the Jewish psyche for generations.

The first experiments in Roman rule were not disastrous. Herod the Great, the client king of Judea between 37 and 4 BCE, was ruthless in the face of any dissent and deeply in thrall to the Romans, but his reign witnessed welcome developments, not least the rebuilding of the Jerusalem Temple, which began in 20/19 BCE. Less popular within the Jewish community was the importation of Roman theaters, amphitheaters, and the entertainments they hosted. Josephus remarked that Jews grumbled about the "conspicuous break with the customs venerated by them. For it appeared a glaring impiety to throw men to wild beasts for the pleasure of spectators." Herod had no desire to launch assaults on Jewish rights in his realm, however, and he even, on occasion, supported the defense of Jewish privileges elsewhere in the empire. In 14 BCE, one of Herod's ministers, Nicolaus of Damascus, spoke passionately, with Herod's blessing, about the undermining of Jewish protections in Asia Minor under the rule of Marcus Agrippa. He talked of their being "deprived of the monies sent as offerings to Jerusalem and of being forced to participate in military service and civic duties and spend their sacred money on these things, although they had been exempted from these duties because the Romans had always allowed them to live in accordance with their own laws."

Subsequent rulers did not always adopt the same attitude. Upon Herod's death, his three sons divided his realms. One of

"Herod the Great, the client king of Judea between 37 and 4 BCE, was ruthless in the face of any dissent and deeply in thrall to the Romans, but his reign witnessed welcome developments"

them, Herod Antipas, ruled over Galilee and Peraea and, as John the Baptist would discover, he was not always tolerant of innovative devotional trajectories within Judaism. Worse yet was Archelaus, who took charge of Samaria, Judaea, and Idumaea. His rule become so unpopular that Rome was forced to remove him and instead established direct rule over his territories. Notably, though, this move was provoked, at least in part, by complaints from the Jewish community, which at least demonstrates that Rome could be responsive to criticism. Regrettably, not all the individuals who filled the subsequent role of prefect in Judea were sympathetic towards Jewish needs—with Pontius Pilate, who ruled between 26 and 36 CE, being a notable example. Pilate would, for instance, break the aforementioned convention of not allowing Roman troops to brandish their banners in Jerusalem.

The Jewish population of the region was always conscious of the precariousness of its situation. Contemporary resentments, particularly about the ever-rising tax burdens that resulted from Roman suzerainty, combined with a keen historical memory of how Gentile rule had brought misery in the past. Even at a distance of almost two centuries, the outrages of the Seleucid period and the great Maccabean revolt of 167 BCE still helped define the Jewish world view. Attitudes towards Rome were apt to vary between the different groups within Jewish society. The conservative priestly caste of the Sadducees tended to look more kindly upon Rome than the more progressive lay scholars among the Pharisees. The ascetical Essenes (associated with the Dead Sea Scrolls) were yet further removed.

Radical Musings

Within Jesus' lifetime, more radical opinions about how to confront the Roman presence began to simmer. In 6 CE, for example, Judas the Galilean led resistance to a census (primarily designed to update tax assessments). Judas and his followers attacked the homes of Jews who complied with the census and called for the establishment of a Jewish state that recognized God alone as its king. This revolt was short lived, but such incidents would become increasingly common over the next decades. Judas' own sons, for example, would emerge as leading figures among the so-called Zealots who strove to undermine Roman rule. Before too long, as Josephus reported, with his customary exaggeration, "Judea was full of brigandage. Anyone might make himself king as head of a band of rebels whom he fell in with." Such men, Josephus opined, had a "passion for liberty that is almost unconquerable." Rome still had to commit many more

crimes before resentment boiled over, but even within Jesus' lifetime the road towards the great Jewish anti-Roman rebellion of 66 CE had been embarked upon.

We should not imagine, of course, that the Jews of the Middle East were in a constant state of anxiety or utterly estranged from their Roman overlords. In many parts of the diaspora, Jews were in a small minority and tended to group together in specific parts of a town or city. In Palestine they were the majority population in an manifestly Jewish society. In Jerusalem, the Temple, one of the era's largest and reputedly most beautiful edifices, dominated the skyline: its rituals and sacrifices, and the public meetings held in its courtyards, provided the pulse beat of Jerusalem's daily life. Against this, stood the conspicuous presence of Roman troops, and it was irksome to have the Roman authorities constantly interfering with the election of the Temple's high priest: a key political, as well as devotional, office.

The emperor Augustus, who passed edicts protecting Jewish rights across the empire

"Attitudes towards Rome were apt to vary between the different groups within Jewish society"

Herod the Great, the ruler of Judea in the decades before the birth of Jesus

A Roman bust of
Pompey the Great,
created during the
reign of Augustus

Roman Views of Judaism

What, though, did the Romans make of the Jewish people? It is certainly possible to locate examples of writers launching into decidedly unpleasant diatribes against the Jews. Cicero had conceded that "each state has its own religious scruples" but the Jews' "practice of their sacred rites was at variance with the glory of our empire, the dignity of our name, the customs of our ancestors." Later, Tacitus would bark that Jews believed "everything is profane which we hold in reverence, and what is permissible with them is abhorrent to us." Jews only kept the Sabbath "because indolence was attractive," their customs "are sinister and abominable and owe their vigor to their depravity." Jews "display only enmity and hatred" towards outsiders and there was a

A Roman gold goblet depicting Jewish ritual objects

"The all-too familiar trope of Jews spreading like locusts was, according to Josephus, relished by Roman writers"

"strong proclivity of the race to lust." The all-too familiar trope of Jews spreading like locusts was, according to Josephus, relished by Roman writers who made up tales of Judaism making "its way into every city" and complained that "it is not easy to find any place in the habitable world which has not taken this race in and which it does not dominate."

There was much mockery of Judaism, though this usually derived from a sense of puzzlement at the things that made Jewish life unique. The Romans could never understand the ritual dietary rules (especially the refusal to eat pork) or the practice of circumcision (dismissed by many writers as pointless mutilation). Such attitudes derived from ignorance, which is hardly excusable, but it would be unfair to suppose that the whole of Roman society was pervaded by rabid anti-Semitism. Some authors exhibited genuine curiosity about the detail of Jewish life.

During the 1st century, many misfortunes and insults would befall the Jewish people. In 19 CE the emperor Tiberius would expel the Jews from the city of Rome itself. Caligula would hatch scandalous plans (happily never realized) to erect a statue of himself inside the Jerusalem Temple. By 70 CE, Roman-Jewish relations would lie in tatters and that very Temple would be destroyed. At least sometimes, however, the Romans had taken their commitment to protecting Jewish rights very seriously. In 38 CE Alexandria's Jewish community endured a horrific pogrom. The emperor Claudius was not best pleased. Writing in 41 CE, he urged the Gentile population "to show humanity and good will towards Jews who have been living in the same city with them

for many generations and not to do anything to desecrate the practices connected with the cult of their god." The "disastrous, outrageous frenzy against one another" must come to an end. The limits of imperial protection were also on display, however. When it came to Alexandria's Jews, "I tell them straight out, not to waste time working for any more privileges than they had before." Moreover, Claudius, according to some ancient sources, conducted his own banishments of Jews from the city of Rome later in his reign. Such was the tension between acceptance and exclusion that pervaded the Jewish world at the time of Jesus, and which had such a profound impact on Jesus' ministry and its reception.

Flavius Josephus

Reliable sources for the relationship between Rome and Judaism are frustratingly scarce. The works of Flavius Josephus, while flawed in many ways, have taken on great significance largely because they happened to survive. Josephus was born in Jerusalem in 37 CE and came to prominence during the Roman-Jewish wars beginning in 66 CE. At first, he fought against the Romans but switched his allegiance to the emperor Vespasian and then Titus: he would even serve as Titus's translator during the siege of Jerusalem. Josephus headed to Rome, was granted Roman citizenship, and embarked upon a second career as a historian. His main works, The Jewish Wars and Antiquities of the Jews, are crammed with bias and inaccuracy, but they also offer many precious details about Jewish history, culture, language, law, and religion. It seems likely that Josephus aimed at a Gentile audience but his books appear to have had a limited impact on the Roman intelligentsia. Nonetheless, they offer rare insights into the world of 1st-century Judaism and they form part of the corpus of works on which any historian of the period relies. ■

A medieval manuscript version of Josephus' works

The hippodrome in Caesarea, built by Herod the Great to host games in honor of the emperor

A Messianic Age

Jewish hopes for the coming of a Messiah had percolated for centuries. How did Jesus fit into this tradition, and did he see himself as the long-awaited savior of Israel?

WRITTEN BY JON WRIGHT

The word Messiah (Mashiach in Hebrew) means "the anointed one" and in earlier Judaism was routinely applied to kings and high priests. It evolved into a term denoting a redeemer who, during a time of great crisis, would appear in Israel, ensure the faithful observance of Jewish law, and establish God's kingdom. A joyous, peaceful era would ensue, and those Jews languishing in exile would return to their ancestral lands. This concept crops up frequently in the Hebrew Scriptures, though we should not assume that understandings of the potential Messiah were uniform or unchanging. He could, by turns, be conceived as a priest or a layman, a prophet or a military champion.

One stream of Messianic thought does, however, appear to have become dominant by the time of Jesus. King David had long been lionized as the epitome of just and fruitful rule, and the notion of one of his descendants playing a transformative role in Jewish history can readily be located in Hebrew Scripture, from the prophets to the Psalms. A branch from the trunk of Jesse, David's father, would endure and at some point there would "come forth . . . one who is to rule in Israel, whose origin is from of old, from ancient days" (Micah 5:2). Or, as the Psalms of Solomon, put it, God would "raise up for them their king, the son of David" who would "reign over Israel . . . that he may shatter unrighteous rulers, and purify Jerusalem of the nations which trample her down in destruction." He would "smash the sinners' arrogance like a potter's vessel" (Psalms of Solomon 17:23).

Messianic musings had not always been an obsession and, between the 5th and 2nd centuries BCE, they played a significant but easily overstated role in Jewish thought. The concept of a Messiah typically came to the fore in times of turmoil, when hopes of better days became a much-needed source of solace. This was clearly the case in the period following Roman intrusion into Palestine in the second half of the 1st century BCE. These Psalms of Solomon were probably composed in the immediate wake of Rome's invasions and, by the first decades of the 1st century CE, benedictions composed for synagogue use talked of "the branch of David soon sprouting forth."

Scholars argue with gusto over whether specific figures during the 1st century CE adopted deliberately Messianic personas to rally support and further their cause. The notion of a Messiah was undoubtedly in the air: it permeated the thought of the Essenes and the Dead Sea Scrolls, for instance. It

A medieval Book of Hours depicts the anointing of Jesus's feet

Jesus portrayed as "Christ pantocrater" the all-powerful ruler of all things, seen here at the Cathedral of Monreale in Sicily

Pieter Coecke van Aelst the Elder depicts Christ's entry into Jerusalem in a painting from the 1530s

a Messianic role. In some instances, the rebels adopted the mantle of a king, even being crowned, and they claimed to be promoting freedom from oppression and the inauguration of a new and better world. Athronges was even a humble shepherd—providing an obvious comparison with David. All told, however, the jury is, and likely always will be out when it comes to deciding whether we should see this cluster of men as aspiring Messiahs.

A similar adjudication applies to figures later in the century. In 44 CE, Theudas introduced himself as a prophet who, before several hundred followers, declared that he could part the waters of the River Jordan. At the time of the Jewish revolt, beginning in 66 CE, several leaders styled themselves as heroes who would liberate the Jewish people. Menahem stormed fortresses and advanced on Jerusalem in decidedly king-like fashion. More charismatic still was Simon bar Giora who was invited into to Jerusalem to protect the city in 69 CE where he minted copper coins that announced the "liberation of Zion". Following Jerusalem's fall, he even went so far as appearing before the Roman authorities in purple (hence regal) robes to provoke his arrest and subsequent execution. But even with these figures clear, obvious Messianic intent is difficult to establish.

Jesus as Messiah

On the face of things, it is much easier to fit Jesus into the category of the potential Messiah. Biblical narratives show that he was viewed as such by his followers. Nonetheless, many historians have suggested potential discrepancies between what the Gospels reported after the fact and what actually transpired. Did Jesus truly see himself as Messiah? Did his supporters? Many incidents in the Gospels support the assertion that they did. We see Christ triumphantly entering Jerusalem and the crowds chanting "Hosanna to the son of David" (Matthew 21:9) and "Blessed is the coming of the kingdom of our ancestor David" (Mark 11:10). We have Christ's feet being anointed (a crucial Messianic word) at Bethany, and Jesus does not object when his closest allies situate him as a redeemer: "You are the Messiah," says Simon Peter, "the son of the living God" (Matthew 16:16). In John the Baptist, Jesus even has an equivalent of the prophet Elijah, often identified as a forerunner of the great redeemer, and the trial before the Sanhedrin revolves around the question of whether Jesus is claiming to be the Messiah.

Some scholars would nonetheless insist that the obvious stress on Christ's Messianic identity was largely a creation of the early Church: that the narrative was shaped to fit the profile after Jesus' death. Throughout

is, though, terribly difficult to pin down the precise objectives and postures of individuals who are sometimes identified as representing themselves in Messianic roles. We must rely on inference rather than certainty.

Candidates abound: Simon of Perea, a former servant or slave of Herod, who set about burning various royal palaces in the first decade of the 1st century CE; Judas of Galilee, who, at around the same period, led a revolt following the announcement of a Roman census; and Athronges who, alongside his four brothers, led attacks against Roman troops and those Jews who were perceived as overly compliant with the Roman regime. The trouble with all these characters is that, while pursuing manifestly radical goals, they do not appear to have specifically claimed

the New Testament, Jesus' Davidic ancestry is taken for granted and repeatedly highlighted. The very application of the Greek word Christos ("the anointed one") to Jesus is clearly intended to demonstrate Jesus' unique role. Much energy, especially in Matthew, is expended on the task of drawing parallels between events in Jesus' life and predictions or foreshadowings in the Hebrew Scriptures. Jesus is the fulfilment of the ancient Messianic story.

None of this diminishes, in the least, the beliefs of those who cherish Jesus' salvific role but, purely as matter of historical certainty, it remains frustratingly difficult to determine whether Jesus ever explicitly declared himself to be the Messiah during his lifetime. If he did, and this is most certainly possible, he was a rather different sort of Messiah. As the Gospels, particularly Luke, recount, Jesus' vision of transformation was unusually pacific. Far from being a great militarily leader with an army at his back, he

John the Baptist recognizes Jesus as the Messiah, in an eighteenth-century engraving by Francesco Bartolozzi

"Some would be denounced as opportunists, others would be taken very seriously for a while, but all would be declared to be false Messiahs"

entered Jerusalem on an ass: a conspicuous parallel, interestingly, with predictions of the Messiah in Zechariah.

Not that any of this calmed the fears of the Jewish authorities. Throughout the 1st century, those who portrayed themselves as the Messiah were treated with skepticism. The theological bar of proof was, for one thing, set very high and, secondly, there were fears that the arrival of someone claiming to be a redeemer set on turning the world upside down was likely to infuriate Rome. This is clearly the logic that was behind the trial and handover of Jesus as portrayed in the Gospel narrative.

It did not, however, extinguish Jewish hopes for a Messiah and, as relations with Rome deteriorated over the remainder of the first century and beyond, Messianic ideas enjoyed something of a resurgence. Notably, Roman emperors also continued to fear a descendant of David becoming the focus of Jewish resistance. One contemporary reports that Vespasian "ordered a search to be made of all the family of David, that there might be left among the Jews no-one of the royal family."

This did not eliminate Messianic expectations and, by the 2nd century, Simon bar Kokhba, leader of the anti-Roman rebellion of 132 to 135 CE, was able, with some success in certain quarters, to announce himself as the true Messiah. Indeed, this would be a recurrent theme in Jewish history which stretched far beyond the ancient era. From David Alroy in the 12th century to Sabbatai Zevi in the 17th, and to Jacob Frank in the 18th, figures would continue to claim the Messianic role. Some would be denounced as opportunists, others would be taken very seriously for a while, but all would eventually be declared to be false Messiahs by the Jewish mainstream.

Jesus, of course, is a case apart. Confidence that he was the true Messiah created a vibrant world-girdling religion although, at the same time, it contributed to a fault line between Judaism and Christianity that would endure for centuries.

The prophet Elijah, often identified as the forerunner of the Messiah

Simon bar Kokhba

It is hard to determine who did and who did not aspire to the role of Messiah during the 1st century CE, but matters become much clearer with the arrival of Simon bar Kokhba, leader of the anti-Roman rebellion of 132-135 CE. Roman rule had become increasingly draconian: plans were afoot to establish a brand-new city, replete with pagan temples, on the site of Jerusalem, and the most cherished Jewish practices, including circumcision, had come under fire. Simon's rebellion, which involved hundreds of thousands of men (all strong enough to uproot a cedar tree, according to legend) secured many victories but was eventually snuffed out by the generals of emperor Hadrian. Rome's reprisals were severe: more than one source talks of children being wrapped in the scrolls of the Torah and being burned alive. Simon clearly attempted to identify himself as the Messiah and was acknowledged as such by some leading rabbis. His adopted surname meant "son of the star," referencing a Messianic prophecy that "a star will shoot forth from Samuel" (Numbers 24: 17). He issued coins bearing a symbol of this star, alongside an inscription announcing "the first year of the redemption of Israel." Others were deeply skeptical and gave Simon the alternative surname bar Kozeba—the son of "the lie" or of "disappointment." ∎

Simon bar Kokhba depicted on the Knesset Menorah in Jerusalem

© Deror avi; Heritage Images / Getty

One Jesus, Four Gospels

Who was Jesus? What was he? Or, as church-goers might ask, who is he now? The Bible's Gospels tell us four distinct and gripping stories

WRITTEN BY ROBIN GRIFFITH-JONES

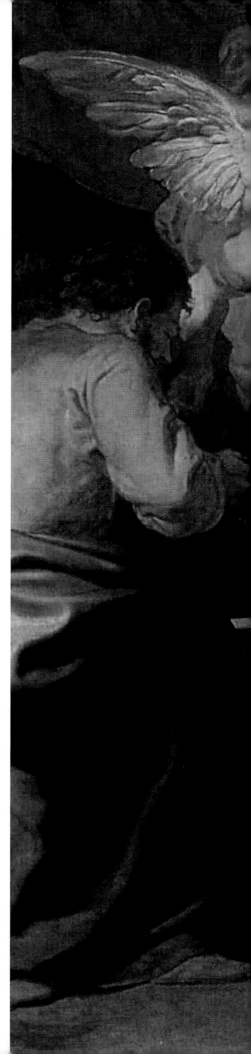

Mark the Rebel

Mark's account of Jesus is short, impetuous, fast-moving. His Greek is clumsy, his story simple; but he has arranged it with masterly care. At its start, Jesus' disciples bask in their master's triumphs: he heals, he teaches, he walks on water, he feeds thousands with a handful of bread.

At the mid-point of the narrative, Mark changes key. Jesus asks openly the question that informs the whole Gospel: "Who do you say I am?" (Mark 8:29). Peter declares Jesus to be God's anointed agent, the Messiah or Christ, and in the next sentence, for the first time, Jesus speaks of his impending rejection and death. Opposition, determined and dangerous, grows closer—Jesus' disciples dream blindly on of both privilege and power, but when put to the test, they run away.

The Gospel darkens. Mark's Jesus seemingly dies in despair: "My God, my God," he cries, "why have you abandoned me?" (Mark 15:34). Jesus' following is scattered, his battle lost. We expect any such defeat to be turned into victory on Easter Day. But in Mark's Gospel, as Mark seems to have planned it, we never quite get this turn. Three women come to Jesus' empty tomb, see an angel, hear that Jesus is risen and run away in terror—and that's it. Here, the Gospel ends.

We cannot be sure of the context in and for which this story was written, but we have a clue. Mark was said to have been the helper and scribe of Simon Peter, leader of Jesus' disciples. Peter was killed in Rome in the persecution that followed the fire of 64 CE. Half the city—the capital of the empire—was destroyed in the flames. Ugly rumors spread that the emperor Nero himself was to blame for the fire. Nero must deflect the blame. The Christians in Rome had been living undisturbed, but they were not popular; they took no part in the pagan rites around them and they murmured about their Jesus as a rival "emperor." The edict was issued: the Christians had lit the fires, so arrest them.

Nero laid on a festival. In an arena, he had the Christians dressed in animal pelts and torn to pieces by lions. Around the arena, he had the Christians hung up on crosses, and covered in pitch. As daylight faded, the crosses were set alight. Where was the triumph of this Jesus now?

Jesus had spoken over and again of "the Son of the Human." For Greek-speakers, this figure was familiar only from a vision of Heaven seen centuries before and recorded in the Bible's book of the prophet Daniel (Dan. 7). This Son of the Human represented, in God's court, God's own obedient people and their ultimate triumph over oppression. Mark's great claim will have dawned gradually on the terrified Christians in Rome. Their Jesus had been this heavenly Son of the Human; he had—unimaginably—come down to Earth and suffered as they were now suffering, and had been invested with all the power that would in the end be theirs. There was a brighter light shining in their darkness than they could yet see.

The Four Evangelists, by Rubens, 1614. Each has his symbol, drawn from a vision in Revelation (7.4): Luke, a bull; Matthew, a man; Mark, a lion; and John, an eagle

Tintoretto, circa 1565, depicts the theft of Mark's body from Alexandria to Venice. Mark with his lion became Venice's patron saint

Matthew the Rabbi

From the violent, restless story of an émigré, to the architectural dignity of Matthew's Gospel, composed in an ancient and distinguished Jewish community. Matthew's Gospel draws on Mark's. It was probably written in Antioch in Syria, due north from Jerusalem along the Levantine coast.

Matthew offers us a stately, commanding Jesus. We hear of Jesus' miraculous conception and of his birth, of Jesus as the promised Emmanuel—"God is with us"—and of the Wise Men's visit and gifts. This Jesus delivers the Sermon on the Mount, the essence of all his teaching compiled into one long speech (Matt. 5-7): "Blessed are the poor in spirt . . ."; "In your prayers, say, 'Our Father in heaven . . .'" He tells of the sheep who are saved the Last Judgment and the goats who are condemned (Matt. 25:31-46). This Jesus dies in apparent despair, as in Mark's story, but from Matthew we hear of the risen Jesus, invested with all power, who commands his disciples to baptize all nations, "and I am with you always, to the end of the age" (Matt. 28:20).

Matthew searches the Jewish scriptures for clues to the identity and standing of Jesus. Was Jesus a leader like Moses, bringing his people out of slavery into some Promised Land? In the Sermon on the Mount, Jesus teaches obedience to Moses' Law—and in the next breath, it seems, on his own authority rewrites it. Was Jesus somehow a new Israel, overcoming the temptations in the desert to which the old Israel had succumbed? But where does this leave the Israel of old, declared by God to be his own people, his child?

Matthew invokes such questions, but he needs more. His Jesus is not just supremely wise; he is the Wisdom of God in human form. His name Emmanuel, as the Gospel's state, proclaims that in him, "God is with us." His closing words after the resurrection: "I am with you" in all power, overcome any distinction between himself and God.

In 66 CE the Jews of Israel had rebelled against Roman rule. For four years they fought on. When, at last, the Romans captured Jerusalem, the Temple itself was set alight and the holy city was left in ruins. In the following years, all the empire's Jews must surely unite in mutual support. But at this very time, the question of Jesus was demanding attention in the synagogues. His followers proclaimed themselves to be the 'real' Israel of God's choosing. Many were Jewish, but Gentiles were attracted to this sect too. Some of the sect's leaders were loyal to the Jewish Law, others not. Either

St. Trophime, circa 1100, Arles, France. Christ sits in judgment and blessing over the church's main entrance, surrounded by symbols of the evangelists

way, all were claiming to have been given authority over their community direct from Jesus himself.

There was increasing bitterness. Worshippers were divided. Did they belong in the synagogues, in the church, or both? Matthew sets out to persuade, cajole, and, if necessary, to threaten his readers out of the synagogues and into loyalty to this newly established church alone. The result has ever since been double-edged: what Matthew wrote to win a local dispute with the synagogues, later churches have used to fuel a terrible anti-Semitism.

Luke the Chronicler

What, then, of Luke? Here we read a story of grand adventure: a vast cast of characters, men and women both rich and poor, a wonderfully elaborate story of Jesus' conception and birth, and a far less harrowing account of his death. Luke writes two volumes, the Gospel and the Acts of the Apostles, for the Gentile powers that be and for imperial officials worried by what they hear of this new sect spreading across the Mediterranean westwards from their empire's eastern fringe. He purports to dedicate his books to "Your Excellency Theophilus," a Roman imperial official (Luke 1:3-4, Acts 1:1). Luke adopts a gracious, literary style; he casts his story in a mold that his cultured readers would recognize, respect, and enjoy. Luke's story is the most immediately attractive of the four. His Jesus is sympathetic and generous. Here are the great stories told by Jesus of the Good Samaritan, the Prodigal Son, and the Rich Man and Lazarus (Luke 10:29-37, 15:11-32, 16:19-31). This Jesus dies with confidence in God and with forgiveness for

Jesus and the Gnostic Gospels

In 1945 a cache of 'gospels' was discovered in an earthenware jar near Nag Hammadi, Egypt; they are written in Coptic. They had been hidden some 1,600 years before. Among the surviving documents, the Gospels of Thomas, Philip, and Mary have attracted widespread attention. They give Mary Magdalene a major role; they come from 'Gnostic' Christians, suppressed by the major churches; they are uncontaminated by those churches' later doctrines. These gospels seemed, then, to bring back to view a more real Jesus, a fresher, less distorted Christianity, and heroic victims of the churches' oppression.

Sadly, not so. Most of these texts, written in the second and third centuries, tell of the risen Jesus who had escaped all the squalour of the flesh and would help his 'Gnostic' followers to do the same. The texts are as artfully composed as the biblical Gospels. What mattered was the knowledge ('gnosis') that this Jesus could impart to the few spiritual souls who were able to be saved. These souls, seen as female, longed for spiritual union with their male savior Christ. The rest of humanity, sunk in its crude longing for sex and the material world, was—with the whole physical universe—beyond redemption.

This ancient Gnosticism is chilling. What we should rescue is the battle we can trace there between women who claimed authority and male leaders who opposed them. Stories of authoritative, insightful 'female' souls inspired—and were perhaps inspired by actual women who sought similar authority in their own churches. ∎

The end of The Gospel of Thomas and start of The Apocryphon of John. A double page from the Nag Hammadi books ('codices'), written in Coptic

"Was Jesus a leader like Moses, bringing his people out of slavery into some Promised Land?"

his enemies (Luke 23:33-46), and on the evening of Easter Day two of his followers, in a long poetic scene, meet the risen Jesus in the dusk and quite fail at first to recognize him (Luke 24:13-35).

Luke sees in Jesus an infinitely attractive example. And over and again the words and actions that Luke records of Jesus are matched by Luke's own comments, by his take on the story. The convergence of such a historian and his hero makes of Luke's account our most appealing Gospel.

Of all our Gospels, Luke's reads most like a chronicle, a straightforward narrative about a historical world such as we inhabit. Yet Luke has an agenda. Thoughtful people had sharp questions to ask. New religions were deeply suspect; the church had abandoned its roots in that ancient Judaism of which the whole empire knew; Jesus' followers were known for their fierce language of freedom and a world turned upside down. Beneath Luke's gracious writing there is an urgent need to reassure such readers as Theophilus that this Jesus and his followers were no threat to Rome.

Our Luke sounds so complaisant, so urbane. Has he lost the hard edge of Mark and Matthew's vision? Far from it. Luke flags up the most inflammatory language of the early church—and transforms it. His Jesus is no threat to Rome, but brings a revolution nonetheless. Luke's reader is not invited to just observe this story, but to sit back and enjoy its adventure. Journeys are under way: Jesus' journey then from Galilee to Jerusalem, and now the reader's own. Here for the reader is a journey into understanding, commitment, and the strange 'revolution' that Luke's Jesus brings.

John the Mystic

With John we enter a different world. Gone are the short, sharp stories and brisk one-liners of our other Gospels' Jesus. Now we have a few elaborate scenes followed by long, spiraling discussions. John's Jesus concludes his public teaching with a climactic miracle: he raises his friend Lazarus from death. The crowd is enthusiastic, while the authorities are frightened—and their maneuvers are under way that will lead to Jesus' death.

To do justice to his Jesus, John takes the reader right back to the dawn of creation. When God created, he said "Let there be light." That Word of God was his self-expression, plan, will, and presence—and Jesus is that Word, in human form. There is a mystery here too deep for normal human understanding. John is convinced that to have any hope of comprehension the reader must be transformed, brought to "new birth" into a spiritual life. In the boldest strategy of all, John sets out to induce that rebirth in the very course of the reader's reading. John is the midwife of the spirit. No wonder his book was already, by the 3rd century, called "the spiritual Gospel."

A cripple is healed; a blind man regains his sight; Lazarus is raised from the dead— each of these stories tells of a single figure. Each tells, too, of the reader, for it is the readers who are drawn through healing and sight to new life, and who hear the

"Our Luke sounds so complaisant, so urbane. Has he lost the hard edge of Mark and Matthew's vision?"

The Last Supper, by Leonardo da Vinci, 1520. Young John, on Jesus' right, has been reclining on Jesus' chest; he is now leaning to the right to hear Simon Peter. Judas Iscariot sits between them

climactic command of Jesus echoing in their tomb, "Lazarus, come on out."

"Let there be light," said the God of Genesis on day one of creation—and creation was under way, of day and night, land and sea, vegetation, animals, and humankind. Adam was entrusted with the Garden of Eden, to tend it, to name its creatures and so to finish their creation. On day six of creation, God completed all his works. And thereafter God, at one with humankind, would walk in the garden in the cool of the day. However, a serpent spoiled the garden; and into the garden where Jesus was came the traitor, a tool of Satan.

Everything, in John's mystical vision, comes full circle. As Jesus dies on Friday, the week's day six, he declares: "It is completed." The new creation is finished. On Easter morning, day one of the new week, very early, when it is still dark, Mary Magdalene weeps outside the empty tomb. She turns and sees Jesus, but she thinks that he is the gardener. He calls her by her name. 'Eve' is once more in Eden; with an 'Adam' who far transcends any human being. He is the God who had once walked in Eden at the cool of the day. He is once

more at one with humankind. No serpent lurks. All creation is made new, and its occupants are John's own readers.

Mark, Matthew, Luke and John: Who Were They?

Within a century of the death of Jesus, Christians were writing about our Gospels and their writers. Behind those names stand decades of editing and refinement that brought the Gospels to their present form.

Mark

We hear in The Acts of the Apostles of John Mark linked with his Cypriot cousin Barnabas (4:36, Col. 4.10), with Simon Peter (Acts 1:12), and with Paul (12:25). At one point, John Mark abandoned Paul and Barnabas to go back to Jerusalem (13:13), and when Barnabas later suggested that he should rejoin them on their mission, Paul refused. There was an argument. John Mark and Barnabas went off to Cyprus (15:39). Paul was at some point reconciled with John Mark (Col. 4:10).

We then hear of "my young Mark" with Peter again in the hated "Babylon," a thin disguise for Rome (1 Peter 5:13). Before 125

CE we hear from Bishop Papias: "Mark was Peter's interpreter; he wrote down accurately but not in order all that he remembered of the Lord's sayings and doings. Mark had not heard the Lord, nor been a follower of his, but later of Peter." (*Commentary on the Lord's Sayings*) We cannot be sure if Papias was right—there was, after all, every reason to discover or create a link between the Gospel and Jesus' greatest disciple.

Matthew

We hear in Matthew's own Gospel that Jesus, "passing by, saw a man called Matthew seated at the tax-desk, and says to him, 'Follow me', and he got up and followed him." (Matt. 9:9) The Gospel then specifies Matthew as the disciple who made his living out of tax-collection (Matt. 10:3). Matthew's story of this call is indebted to Mark's account of a similar incident, when "Levi" was called (Mark 2:13). It may be that Matthew was a Levite, and was known by both names.

Did this disciple write or edit the Gospel that bears his name? Our earliest evidence is again in Papias' commentary on the Lord's Sayings: "Matthew in the Hebrew

Josephus and Jesus

Josephus, greatest of the ancient Jewish historians, wrote briefly about Jesus around 93-4 CE. "About this time," reads Josephus' present text, "there lived a man Jesus, a wise man, if one really ought to call him a man at all. For he was one who did extraordinary works, a teacher of such people as accept truths gladly, and he won over many Jews and many of the Greeks. He was the Christ. On the accusation of leading men among us, Pilate condemned him to be crucified; but those who had come in the first place to love him did not cease to do so. For he appeared to them on the third day as alive again; and the prophets of God had prophesied these and countless other marvelous things about him. And the nation of the Christians has still to this day not disappeared." (*Antiquities* 18.3.3)

Scholars have long distrusted this eulogy. Perhaps, before a Christian editor got to work on the text, Josephus really said: "About this time, there lived a man Jesus, a clever man. He was one who did strange deeds, a teacher of such people as accept novelties too readily, and he led astray many Jews and many of the Greeks. On the accusation of leading men among us Pilate condemned him to be crucified. And the tribe of the Christians has still to this day not disappeared." ■

Josephus wrote our fullest account of the Jewish rebellion against Rome, 66-70 CE. Rome's Arch of Titus shows the booty taken from the Temple when Jerusalem fell

Russian icon of Luke painting the Virgin Mary. Luke was in later tradition an artist; a likeness of Jesus or Mary supposedly by Luke had eye-witness authority

"This Hebrew—or rather, Aramaic—Gospel of Matthew is intriguing"

language arranged the sayings, and each person translated them as best he could." This Hebrew—or rather, Aramaic—Gospel of Matthew is intriguing. No trace of it has survived, and our own Greek Gospel of Matthew does not read like a translation. That Aramaic original may indeed be a chimaera. Papias' crucial sentence about Matthew could be translated as such: "Matthew organized the sayings in the style used in Jewish writings."

Luke

"Luke," we read at the end of one Pauline letter, "the much-loved physician, sends his greetings." (Col. 4:14) And again: "Luke alone is with me." (2 Tim. 4:10) Some passages in Acts are written in the first person plural, as if by someone who shared Paul's journeys: "On the first day of the week," for example, "We met for the breaking of bread together . . ." (Acts 20:7) It would be easy to imagine that these were entries in a diary incorporated by their own writer, Paul's sole companion, into a chronicle he wrote, but it is impossible to prove. We might question such an attribution to Luke that so advantageously lent Paul's authority to the books.

'Luke' is a Greek version of a Latin name. Luke may have been Jewish; a former slave—perhaps his master's highly educated

Graham Sutherland's great tapestry in Coventry Cathedral, 1962, shows Christ surrounded by the same symbols in modern, abstract form

secretary—might well have adopted his Gentile master's name. But whether Jewish or Gentile, Luke inhabits the Gentile world and knows it well. He is attuned to its sensibilities; and is perhaps the Gospels' best envoy to all those readers who are Gentiles themselves.

John

An unnamed figure in John's Gospel is "the disciple whom Jesus loved." He reclined on Jesus' chest at the supper before Jesus died (John 13:23-4). This disciple saw Jesus' death: "He who saw this has testified to it, and his testimony is truthful, and that man knows that he speaks the truth, so that you too might believe." (John 19:35)

Who was that eye witness? John's next and last chapter has long been seen as an appendix, written by a slightly later author. "The disciple whom Jesus loved is the disciple who is testifying about these things and who wrote them, and we [his own pupils, who preserved his work] know that his testimony is true." (John 21:20)

Eventually this disciple gets an identity: John, perhaps one of the fiery sons of Zebedee (Mark 3:17, 10:35; Luke 9:54). John, we are told, lived at Ephesus until the reign of Trajan, emperor from 98 CE. As a young man, Polycarp, who died in 156 CE, spent time with John. Irenaeus, writing around 190, heard Polycarp speak of him. Irenaeus tells us, "Later John the Lord's disciple who reclined on the Lord's chest himself published the Gospel while staying at Ephesus in Asia." Perhaps our Gospel, through to its completion, really was under the direction of "the disciple whom Jesus loved."

The Book of Kells, a 9th century illuminated manuscript, depicts the four evangelists. Clockwise from top left: Matthew is represented by a man, Mark by a lion, John by an eagle, and Luke by a calf

Jesus: Son of Mary—and 'Son of God'?

Visions, dreams, the angel Gabriel, shepherds, and three Wise Men: the events surrounding Jesus' birth were enough to bewilder any parents. But what does the scripture really say about the event?

WRITTEN BY ROBIN GRIFFITH-JONES

Books begin as they mean to go on. The opening pages set the tone, and get the readers into the right mood for all that follows. Of the Bible's four Gospels, only Matthew and Luke tell the famous stories of Christmas, but Mark and John have equally dramatic openings. So we will enjoy all four accounts here—with a natural emphasis on Matthew and Luke.

Jesus was certainly the son of Mary, almost certainly not the son of Joseph, and said by Christians to be the Son of God (even opponents of the ancient church admitted that Joseph was not the father. One story claimed Mary had been with a soldier, Pantera). In the Jewish scriptures, there are psalms and prophecies extolling a king on his enthronement. "I will proclaim the Lord's decree, 'You are my son, today I have begotten you" (Psalm 2:6-7); "The Lord himself said to my own lord, 'Come and sit at my right hand. In sacred splendor, from the womb of the dawn, you have the dew [of generation] with which I have begotten you'." (Psalm 110:1-3) From the moment of enthronement, the new king became such a Son of God, and was invested with God's authority over his kingdom. He was by adoption and appointment God's ambassador and presence on Earth. He was also the embodiment of his own kingdom and all

its subjects. He was, therefore, a sacred figure, an intermediary between God and his people, representing each to the other.

The roles of king and high priest overlapped. In ancient Israel, kings and priests were anointed with oil on their installation; 'the Christ' and 'the Messiah' mean simply, 'the Anointed'. When the high priest put on his robes and entered the temple, he too became a form of god before his people, and of the people before God.

Assyrian kings and Egyptian pharaohs were also declared to be sons of their most important god. The mother of Alexander the Great (died 323 BCE) might have spread the famous story that she had been visited by Zeus, king of the gods, before her marriage to Philip, Alexander's supposed father. Alexander himself notoriously visited a temple of Ammon in Libya and thereafter claimed to be son of Ammon-Re, identified by the Greeks as Zeus. But in general, such divine and human paternity could coexist. It was amongst the early Christians that the title 'Son of God' became the title of Jesus and only Jesus; and conversely, there that Jesus became the Son of God and of God alone. The title and its bearer were rising in importance. Jesus was, as the Christians came to believe, not just son, a son, or the son, but the—one, majestic, eternally begotten—Son of God.

Mystic Nativity, by Botticelli. A joyous illustration of Revelation 12. The 12 angels wheeling in the sky are the 12 stars around the head of the woman clothed with the sun. In the foreground, the Devils are bound

The dove descends from God in golden whorls and sends a spurt of gold into the Virgin's womb through the hole in her tunic

Mary conceives through the ear; the angel had spoken to her, as God created the universe through his Word

The definite article ('the') and capital letters enable us to mark that scale of rising grandeur. But our Greek manuscripts of the New Testament do not distinguish between capital and lower-case letters, and the definite article is more emphatic in Greek than in English and can, when no emphasis is needed, more easily be omitted. Where we can be specific in our description of a son or Son of God, our manuscripts are inescapably—and perhaps very fruitfully—ambiguous.

Paul's Jesus: God's Son at Easter

In 55-6 CE Paul wrote to the Christians in Rome. He did not know them. He opens his letter with a formula of faith which he expects them to know already: he is preaching the Gospel "concerning God's son who, in terms of the flesh, was born as a descendent of King David and, in terms of the spirit of holiness, was designated God's son in power by the resurrection of the dead." (Romans 1:3-4) In this very early creed, then, it seems to have been at the resurrection—at Easter—that Jesus was given the role of God's Son.

This is close to the sequence implied in another early formula, this time in a hymn which Paul quotes to the Philippians in the early 50s or 60s. He himself may have taught it to them when he visited Philippi in 48-9

"In Mark's story, it seems, Jesus is invested with the son's power not at his resurrection, but at his baptism"

CE. Jesus was "in the form of God," and so was already an eternal, heavenly figure, but humbled himself to become human and to die, "and therefore God has highly exalted him, and given him the name above every name, so that at the name of Jesus every knee shall bow, to the glory of God the Father." (Phil. 2:5-10) The name above every name is the name of God himself; and in Judaism all creatures must bow the knee to God and to God alone. This looks like Jesus' promotion after death to a standing far above that which he had before he came to Earth.

When did Jesus become who he finally became? The Christians of those early years were at the start of a long, spell-binding process of thought.

Mark's Jesus: God's Son at Baptism

Mark's Jesus bursts onto the scene, already an adult. Mark shows no interest in his ancestry or birth. Two prophecies and John the Baptist introduce him, then we move straight into the Gospel's first scene: John the Baptist baptizes Jesus in the River Jordan, and as he does the heavens are torn open and a voice declares, "You are my beloved son, in you I have taken delight."

Beyond the heavens, in ancient thought, lies the throne room of God; when the skies were torn open, God's plan and character were miraculously revealed to humankind. In Mark's story, it seems, Jesus is invested with the son's power not at his resurrection (at the end of his work on Earth), but at his baptism (right at its start).

Mark is gripped by Jesus' miracles and teaching, as Paul was not; so Mark needs Jesus to have all of God's authority from the beginning. Within a couple of pages, the demons recognize Jesus as the Holy One of God who threatens their power. And at the story's climax, when Jesus dies, the veil of the temple is torn in two and the Roman centurion in charge of the execution declares, "It's true, this man was God's son!" The temple's veil separated its outer spaces from the innermost sanctuary, the Holy of Holies, which represented on Earth the throne room of God in Heaven; the veil was dark blue, decorated with sun, moon, and stars. When the veil was torn, the 'heavens' were again opened to human view and the whole plan and character of God were revealed—in the death of Jesus.

Mark is overawed by Jesus. This Jesus is not only Son of God, he is also 'the son of

the Human' enthroned by God, as seen in a vision of Heaven by the prophet Daniel; he belongs in Heaven and in dreams, not on Earth as one of us. He is just what one might hope to see if the heavens were torn apart and a view opened into God's court. Mark does not need to worry about Jesus' conception, backwards to his ancestors and forwards to his birth; what matters is Jesus' standing upwards in Heaven and down below on Earth. Mark's story is vertical, not horizontal.

Mark's viewpoint is dazzling. His successors, Matthew and Luke, would need to address more earthbound questions: how did this Jesus relate to his own ancestral Judaism and to the Gentile world beyond it? For answers, they turned to Jesus' forebears and to his birth. We are about to hear the great Christmas stories in their two different forms, told with different aims in mind.

Matthew's Jesus: "A Virgin will Conceive"

Joseph and Mary were engaged, but had not slept together. Mary became pregnant and Joseph planned to call off the marriage, but an angel appeared to him in a dream, telling him he need not worry, for Mary had "conceived what was in her by the Holy Spirit." Joseph and Mary stayed together, and Jesus was born. Here is the first of the well-known Christmas stories.

Amid the grand ruins of the pagan world, the inhabitants of Earth and Heaven bring flowers to Jesus and his mother

The Genealogies of Jesus: and Insolubale Puzzle?

Matthew and Luke both list Jesus' paternal ancestry: Matthew back as far as Abraham, Luke all the way back to Adam and so to God. Abraham was the patriarch of the Jews; but God had also promised that in his descendants "all the nations of the Earth will be blessed." (Gen. 22:18) He is the perfect starting point for Matthew, for whom God's people now potentially includes all the non-Jewish nations of the world. Luke has an even broader vision: the world's whole order was turning on its hinges. Adam, 'Son of God' in the old order, had been created with no human father; and so, in the new, was Jesus. Both Gospels then bring Jesus' ancestry, as they must, through King David; God had promised the throne of Israel to David's descendants (2 Sam. 7, Ps. 89, Ps. 132). Each list is tightly structured. Matthew builds successive groups of 14 generations each; 14 is the numerical value of 'David' (d + w + d = 4 + 6 + 4) in Hebrew. Luke, of seven generations each; seven represented perfection.

Theology, then, was everywhere in these genealogies. But where was history? The Gospels already give us two different names for Joseph's father. And thereafter their lists diverge wildly. One evangelist may have been adapting a reliable family tree, but then the other surely was not. Most intriguing are the four women mentioned by Matthew: Tamar, Rahab, Ruth and the wife of Uriah. All were foreigners, which will have mattered to Matthew; and all furthered God's plan for the great lineage in strange or irregular ways—as Mary would, in the strangest way of all, when she conceived as a virgin. ∎

Can We Believe in the Virgin Birth?

Matthew and Luke tell us that Mary conceived Jesus without the intervention of any human father. She was, after his conception, still a virgin. By the 2nd century there were churches that extended this virginal conception of Jesus to his Virgin Birth. By the 4th century it was becoming commonplace that Mary had remained a virgin, as St. Augustine insisted, "before Jesus' birth, during his birth and forever after his birth." At issue was not simply Mary's virginity, but her single-minded dedication to God's will; she was, as it were, virginal in body and mind alike.

Such reflection on Mary grew in range. Augustine traced the evil within us all to the Fall of Adam and Eve. Somewhere in their proud defiance of God had been an irrational appetite to which they succumbed. Such appetites, in us all, have ever since been represented and realized in sexual desire. No wonder it is, Augustine claimed, through sexual generation that the miasma of the fall has been inescapably passed on through every generation. Jesus was not conceived through sexual congress— he is free from the corruption that it brings. And his mother? She was the new and obedient Eve to Jesus' new Adam. Surely she too must have been free (at conception) or freed (instantly after conception) from any taint of sin.

To believe such claims is now to credit some outdated views of history, biology, and sex. Through most of Christian history, it was primarily to see in Christ a new creation. Those who believe in God's first creation, as described in Genesis, have generally believed in his second. ∎

The Virgin is shown as the woman mystically seen in Revelation 12, clothed with the sun, and with 12 stars around her head and the moon beneath her feet

Jesus lies asleep on his mother's lap, as his body will one day lie again, after the crucifixion

"The Jesus of Matthew and Luke is miraculous from his conception"

And next, the Magi or Wise Men arrive from the East, with their presents of gold, frankincense, and myrrh; they deserve their own separate section, which you can find on page 50.

Matthew rounds off the angel's message: "All this took place to fulfill what the Lord had spoken through the prophet Isaiah," (Isaiah 7:14) "Look, the virgin will be pregnant and will bear a son, and they will call him Immanuel, which means God-with-us." In our secular West, this story of virginal conception is, naturally enough, open to a fair amount of suspicion.

There is an added twist to the tale. Matthew quotes from Isaiah, who wrote in Hebrew some 700 years before. With the royal family or his own in mind, Isaiah used an unusual word for 'young woman' (almā) and not the normal word for 'virgin' (betūlāh). And even if Isaiah meant 'virgin', he was making no special claim. A virginal bride was going to be married, and would then sleep with her husband and conceive. There would be no miracle here.

Matthew, by contrast, knew Hebrew but wrote in Greek. He drew on various versions of the Jewish scriptures. Among them was the standard Greek translation, the Septuagint, made 200-300 years before he wrote. This translated Isaiah's 'young woman' with a word that was almost only ever used for a 'virgin' (parthenos), and this was the translation used here by Matthew. Did Matthew pick a late version of Isaiah and invent the virginal conception simply to get that prophecy fulfilled in Jesus?

The answer to this familiar question is, no. Matthew includes five prophecies from the Jewish scriptures which were fulfilled in the conception, birth, and infancy of Jesus. They are all introduced with the same formula, and they all interrupt the story. They have been inserted by Matthew into a narrative that once ran more smoothly without them. Isaiah's prophecy may well have influenced the story of Jesus; but if so, it was before the story took its present form.

But Matthew makes good use of that prophecy. Isaiah's God-with-us recurs through five chapters of warning, threat, and promise that all revolve around the birth of special children (Isaiah 7-11). Matthew was alerting his readers that in Jesus this whole climactic drama in Israel's history was, 700 years after Isaiah, at last being realized and transcended.

And then Matthew brings God-with-us back into his own story, right at its end. The last words of the Gospel are spoken by Jesus, after his resurrection, to his disciples: "All power in heaven and on Earth has been given to me . . . And look, I am with you always, to the end of time." (Matt. 28:20)—from God-with-us at the start, to I-am-with-you at the end. This was a spine-tingling promise, but vague. What would make Jesus palpably present in Matthew's churches? Matthew re-crafted everything that Jesus had said and done in the 30s CE to address Matthew's own churches as they were in the 80s. The Gospel itself, recited in those churches' services, was no longer just recollections of Jesus; it was the speech and action—the presence of Jesus—then and there.

A dream, an angel, and God-with-us: the virginal conception clearly mattered to Matthew—as part of his whole vast view of the past and present of God's people.

Luke's Jesus: "Hail Mary, Full of Grace!"

The angel Gabriel visited Mary and greeted her, "Hail, Mary, full of grace." Mary laid Jesus in the manger, because there was no room for them in the inn. There were shepherds in the fields at night, and angels brought them the news of Jesus, joyously singing.

These wonderful moments are recorded by Luke alone. They are just a small part of his celebratory story—five times the length of Matthew's—of Jesus' conception and birth. Luke sees two stages in God's dispensation for the world: the old order, centered in Jerusalem and its temple, and the new order, realized in Jesus. In Luke's grand narrative, the new grows out of the old, and (when rightly understood) both confirms and transcends it. There is no hint here of Isaiah's prophecy, deployed by Matthew.

John the Baptist and his cousin Jesus are mirror images of each other: John embodies the old order, Jesus the new. The Baptist's parents were elderly, his mother Elizabeth past child-bearing age. His father Zechariah was a priest in Jerusalem's temple. They represent the best and truest of the old order. Gabriel appears to Zechariah in the temple to tell him that Elizabeth will have a son; Zechariah cannot believe it, and is dumbstruck.

Then Gabriel appears, 100 miles up-country in Galilee, to the young woman Mary, a virgin: she too is to have a son, Jesus, "who will be called son of the Most High." Mary is also incredulous at first, but then confirms, "Let it be to me as you have said." Mary visits Elizabeth, and only when Elizabeth confirms her own pregnancy does Mary break into her famous poem of joy, known in churches as the Magnificat: "My soul proclaims the greatness of the Lord."

Elderly Elizabeth gives birth. Once Zechariah confirms in writing that the boy must be called John, his speech is restored and he in his turn declaims a paean of praise, the Benedictus: "Blessed be the Lord, the God of Israel." Then, greater miracle still, the Virgin Mary gives birth, to Jesus.

The Magnificat and Benedictus seem to promise revolution: Israel will be rescued from slavery, the rich will be sent away hungry, the humble will be exalted. So Luke has the child welcomed by shepherds, who were uneducated and poor. Luke is a strangely brave author. He is writing for the powers that be. He acknowledges the fieriest language of threat and promise used by the Christians, everything that might deepen the suspicions of his audience. Surely these Christians must be suppressed? Not so. The Gospel as a whole will defuse any threat to the Roman order. This sect may be strange, but its members never intended to break from ancient and respected Judaism; and for all their incendiary talk, they can safely be left in peace.

We might think that Luke colluded too closely with Rome; but he alone managed, by his sleight of hand, to preserve those most exhilarating promises of change.

John" "In the Beginning was the Word"

The Jesus of Matthew and Luke is miraculous from his conception. John's Son of God had been in glory with God the Father from the dawn of time; he was God's Word, the eternal, all-creating, all-sustaining plan of God and its perfect expression. John's Gospel begins at the beginning of all things: "In the beginning was the Word." And from that first creation the Gospel itself brings a new creation to birth. Jesus himself is the Word made flesh; and in turn he gives those who trust in him, the audience of John's own Gospel, "the power to become the sons of God." The one and only Son is going to have numberless siblings. All this is declared in the Gospel's opening lines, a hymn that transports its audience halfway to Heaven.

Matthew's Jesus launches and embodies a renewed people of God; Luke's Jesus, God's renewed order for the world; John's Jesus, a whole new creation. It took 60 years or so from Jesus' death for these Gospels to reach their finished form; and it may—we cannot know—have taken all that time for their churches to trace Jesus as the Son of God back to his conception and further still. A skeptic might call this invention; the churches would call it a long, slow process of discovery.

St. Francis of Assisi setting up the Christmas crib at Greccio, fresco in Assisi by Giotto. Francis is said to have been the first to make such a crib

The Virgin's robe of dark heavenly blue extends under Jesus and unites them, an umbilical cord between mother and child, earthly and heavenly

Jesse Tree, Chartres Cathedral, c. 1150

The prophet Isaiah spoke of the descendants of Jesse, father of the great King David: "And there shall come forth a rod out of the stem of Jesse, and a branch shall grow out of his roots. And the spirit of the Lord shall rest upon him, the spirit of wisdom and understanding, the spirit of counsel and might, the spirit of knowledge and of the fear of the Lord; and shall make him of quick understanding in the fear of the Lord. With righteousness shall he judge the poor, and reprove with equity for the meek of the Earth." (Is. 11:1-4) In 12th century Europe royal dynasties were establishing their lineage and with it their legitimacy. Kings were sacred; they drew analogies between Christ's royal ancestry and their own, and so between his wise rule and theirs. A stained-glass window at Chartres is the most famous of all Jesse Trees. From Jesse's reclining figure in the bottom panel springs a tree trunk; in the successive panels, rising up the window, are David, then David's son Solomon, then two generic kings, then the Virgin Mary, and at the top the far larger figure of Christ, surrounded by seven doves for the seven gifts of the spirit listed by Isaiah. Flanking each figure are two small prophets, identified by inscriptions. The central figures are each framed by a white lily-of-the-valley or fleur-de-lys, an emblem both of the French royal line and of the Virgin Mary. Virgin in Latin is "virgo," rod is "virga." The window is a double celebration of Christ and of his mother.

Tree of Jesse by Marc Chagall, 1975.
The Jewish artist Chagall accumulates
motifs from Jewish and Christian
scriptures in a haze of luminous colors

Jesus' Family Tree

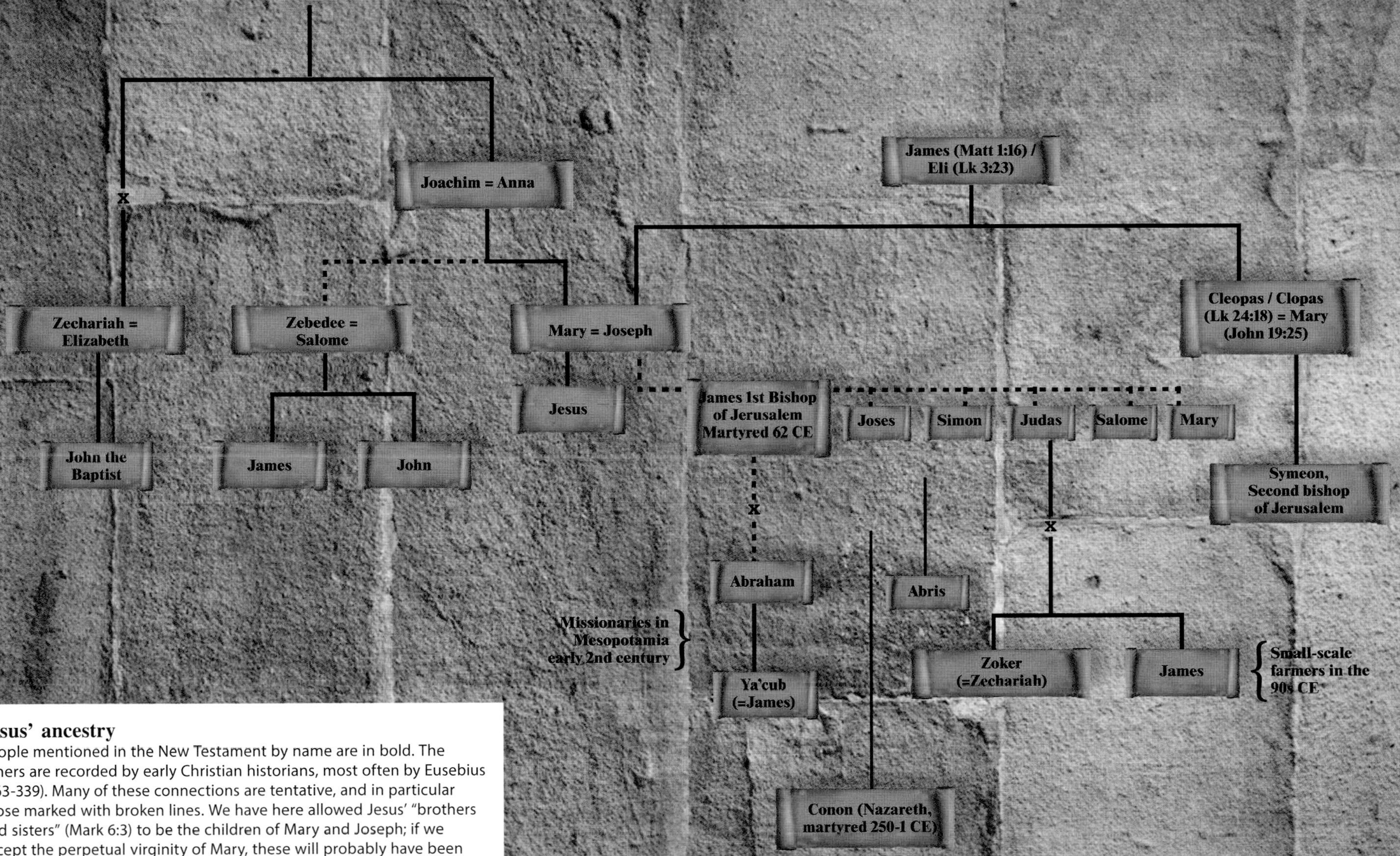

Jesus' ancestry

People mentioned in the New Testament by name are in bold. The others are recorded by early Christian historians, most often by Eusebius (263-339). Many of these connections are tentative, and in particular those marked with broken lines. We have here allowed Jesus' "brothers and sisters" (Mark 6:3) to be the children of Mary and Joseph; if we accept the perpetual virginity of Mary, these will probably have been the children of Joseph by an earlier marriage. I have cautiously allowed three women mentioned in different gospels as being at the crucifixion to be the same person: Salome (Mark 15:40), the mother of the sons of Zebedee (Matt. 27:36) and the sister of Jesus' mother (John 19:25).

Zechariah = Elizabeth

John the Baptist

Zebedee = Salome

James

John

Joachim = Anna

Mary = Joseph

Jesus

Missionaries in Mesopotamia early 2nd century

Abraham

Ya'cub (=James)

Conon (Nazareth, martyred 250-1 CE)

Abris

Zoker (=Zechariah)

James

James 1st Bishop of Jerusalem Martyred 62 CE

Joses

Simon

Judas

Salome

Mary

James (Matt 1:16 / Eli (Lk 3:23)

Cleopas / Clopas (Lk 24:18) = Mary (John 19:25)

Symeon, Second bishop of Jerusalem

Small-scale farmers in the 90s CE

Jesus' Family Tree **47**

The Mystic Nativity
Artist: Sandro Botticelli
Year: c. 1500

In this unexpected painting of the birth of Jesus, Botticelli defies conventional practices for traditional Nativity scenes, instead using motifs that prophesize the fate of Jesus, particularly symbols that proved popular in depictions of the Last Judgement. Among the celebrating audience, demons flee; the baby Jesus rests on the shroud he would later be buried in; while the stable looks more akin to a cave.

"We Three Kings of Orient Are"

The Magi came from the East to see the baby Jesus, bringing gifts of gold, frankincense and myrrh. Who were they, and where from? What was the star they saw, and why did they follow it?

WRITTEN BY ROBIN GRIFFITH-JONES

The most famous story in Matthew's Gospel is of the Magi (Matthew 2:1-12). Far in the east, they saw a star and followed it westwards. It surely portended a king's birth, so when they reached Judea the Magi visited King Herod in Jerusalem. He knew nothing of this apparent rival to his rule. His advisors told him of prophecies that a king would be born in Bethlehem, so he sent the Magi there, asking them to return to tell him where the baby was, "so that I might come and worship him also." The Magi found the child, venerated him, gave him presents of gold, frankincense and myrrh, and went home another way. Just as well. Herod had wanted to locate this new king only in order to kill him; and now, to leave nothing to chance, he massacred all the small boys in Bethlehem. But he missed his intended victim, as Mary and Joseph had already taken the young Jesus to safety in Egypt.

For centuries astronomers had tried to specify the 'star'. What memory might lie behind Matthew's simple word: the appearance of a supernova, a comet, or the conjunction of two or three planets? There are more than enough candidates around the time of Jesus' birth. The great astronomer Johannes Kepler (1571-1630) was already calculating possibilities in the 17th century; he suggested that the star had been a 'new

star' or supernova, but it has been hard to find any record of such an appearance at the right period. Halley's Comet had passed in 12-11 BCE. Jupiter and Saturn were in conjunction three times in 7-6 BCE in the constellation of Pisces; for astrologers, Jupiter was the planet of the world's ruler, Saturn of Syria-Palestine, and Pisces was linked with the Jews and with the end of days. A conjunction of stars, a comet, or a strange sight in the sky: these could all too easily portend a great event, a crisis or a special birth. "A comet blazed into view," records Tacitus of Nero's reign. "About a comet the crowd's view is: it bodes a change of regime. So people asked who would succeed Nero, as if Nero were already dethroned." The Emperor Nero (reigned 54-68 CE) was so alarmed that he fulfilled its portent—by having several of his own grandees put to death. A star stood over Jerusalem and a comet was seen for a whole year as the city fell to the Roman armies in 70 CE.

Astronomy, astrology, divination, and the interpretation of dreams were closely connected in the ancient world, and their experts were widely known as 'Magi'. There are other stories like ours. In 66 CE King Tiridates of Armenia, far to the East, came to Rome with the sons of three neighboring Persian kings to pay homage to the Emperor Nero. Their journey was like

The Magi's relics reached Cologne in 1164. The cathedral built to house them, the largest Gothic cathedral in Northern Europe, took over 600 years to complete

"Bearing Gifts we Traverse Afar"

Matthew's Magi will have come from one of three civilizations to the east. First, Persia. Magi and their mastery of dreams are first recorded in Persia, modern Iran, to the northeast, and most early Christian writers placed our Magi there. A mosaic in the Basilica of the Nativity in Bethlehem even showed them in the belted tunics, trousers, and peaked caps that Persians wore. When the Persians invaded Palestine in 614 CE, they burned down almost every church, but when they saw this mosaic, they spared the Basilica. The Magi's gifts, however, suggest an Arabian origin: gold and frankincense are twice linked in the Bible (Isaiah 60:6 and Psalm 72:15) with Arabian camel trains. And finally, the astrology hints at Babylonia, famous for its astronomy. Many Jews had been taken into exile in Babylon in 587-6 BCE, and a large colony settled there forever.

We nowadays associate gold with divinity, frankincense with prayer, and myrrh with burial. But the key to the gifts might lie in the survival in Babylon of ancient Jewish beliefs that had been lost in Judea. Gold, frankincense, and myrrh had all been used in the Jewish Temple in Jerusalem that the Babylonians had destroyed: the temple's implements were all of gold, only the High Priest burned frankincense, and myrrh anointed the king. Perhaps, with the Magi, ancient stories, hopes, and rituals were being brought back home, from Babylon to Judea, at last. ■

The Magi Journeying by James Tissot, c. 1890, with a more modern emphasis on the hardship of their journey

The Magi in Persian clothes with their familiar names Balthassar, Melchior, and Caspar, mosaic, c. 565, S. Apollinare Nuovo, Ravenna, Italy

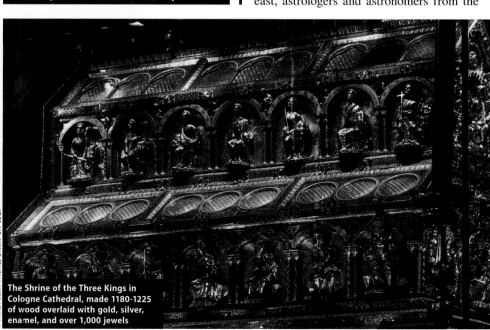

The Shrine of the Three Kings in Cologne Cathedral, made 1180-1225 of wood overlaid with gold, silver, enamel, and over 1,000 jewels

a triumphal procession; all of Rome itself was decorated with lights and garlands, and the rooftops were filled with onlookers. Tiridates identified himself as a descendent of Arsaces, founder of the Persian Empire, and declared to Nero, "I have come to you, my god, to pay homage, as I do to the god Mithras." Nero confirmed him in his kingship; Tiridates and his entourage, we hear, "did not return by the route he had followed in coming," but sailed back by another way. The historian Pliny refers to Tiridates and his companions as Magi (*Natural History* 30.6.17). And in the same year, Halley's Comet appeared.

"Star with Royal Beauty Bright"

Within 20 years Matthew would be writing his Gospel in Syria, not so far from Tiridates' kingdom of Armenia. To typify Gentiles—the wisest, most highly educated Gentiles—who better than Magi from the east, astrologers and astronomers from the ancient civilizations of Persia, Arabia, or Babylon? They come with frankincense and myrrh; both were used in prayers of divination. Matthew does not call them kings, but the Jewish scriptures foretold the homage of kings (Psalm 72:10, Isaiah 60:1-6), so the Magi were soon promoted in Christian interpretation. Nor does Matthew number them, but the classic trio, with one gift each, is now accepted everywhere.

Jewish tradition nursed the prediction of one star as a vital portent. King Balak, determined to destroy the Hebrews arriving in the Holy Land under Moses, commissioned Balaam—from the East—to curse them. But far from it. Balaam is inspired to speak out: "I see him, though not now; I behold him, though he is not near; a star will come forth from Jacob, and a scepter will rise from Israel." (Numbers 24:17)

When the passage was translated into Greek, three centuries before Matthew wrote, its meaning was made more direct: the "scepter" it spoke of became a single "man," a king. Before the time of Jesus the sectaries of Qumran were applying this prophecy to the longed-for Messiah. The Aramaic translations of scripture probably familiar in Jesus' own day paraphrased the passage to make its significance clear: "A king will arise from Jacob, and the Messiah will be anointed from Israel." And at the next and last revolt against the Romans, in 135 CE, the rebels' leader was heralded as the Messiah, and changed his name to show that Balaam's prophecy had been fulfilled at last: he had been simply Bar Kosiba, "Son of Kosiba;" from now on he would be known as Bar Kochba, "Son of the Star." Jesus himself is "the bright Morning Star" (Rev. 22:16) that shines in the east at dawn, bringing light to those in darkness (Luke 1:71-9).

The ancient past was never far away in Jewish thought. Matthew's whole Gospel presents Jesus as a new Moses, who will lead his people out of their present slavery into a new freedom. We know from the Jewish historian Josephus of some stories, current in Matthew's day, about the birth of Moses. Josephus told of the Jews' slavery in Egypt. One of the sacred scribes of Egypt told the Pharaoh that one was due to be born to the Jews who would bring down the rule of the Egyptians and raise up the Jews. Frightened by this, the Pharaoh then ordered that every son born to the Israelites should be thrown in the river and killed. Among the Jews was Amran, whose wife was pregnant. God appeared to him in a dream to reassure him: "This child, whose birth has filled the Egyptians with such fear that they have condemned the Jews' children to death, will indeed be your child; he shall free the Jews from their slavery in Egypt, and will be remembered for as long as time endures." (Antiquities 2.9.2-3) Matthew had every reason to relish such a precedent as he designed his narrative.

"Glorious Now Behold Him Arise"

Within and behind the story we should acknowledge Matthew's own role as author of the Gospel as a whole. He binds it together with motifs that appear at its

start and at its end. Herod in Jerusalem summoned all the chief priests and scribes for advice; and when the adult Jesus reaches Jerusalem for the last time, all the chief priests and the elders will conspire against him. All Jerusalem was thrown into turmoil by the Magi's news; Jerusalem will take the blood of Jesus upon itself and its children. The Magi found Jesus by the light of a star; Jesus will die under a darkened sky. The Magi recognized Jesus as King of the Jews; as King of the Jews he will be mocked on the cross. The Gentile Magi are the first to pay him homage, as an infant; the Gentile centurion, seeing him die, will declare him Son of God. A silent Joseph protected the infant Jesus from Herod's attack; a second Joseph, of Arimathaea, just as silent in the story, will secure the body of Jesus and will bury him.

We hear of the Magi at Christmas, among the lovely stories of Jesus' birth and infancy. We may well find it strange in itself. No normal star could be identified

"The Jewish scriptures foretold the homage of kings, so the Magi were soon promoted in Christian interpretation"

directly above Jerusalem and then, after moving, above a particular building five miles away. And in general we distrust stories that have been so clearly shaped to promote their author's agenda. Matthew did indeed build the Magi into the architecture of his Gospel, and with them set the Gospel's tone: at once fueled by the heroes and prophecies of the Jewish scriptures, and attuned to the political dramas of his own day. In Jesus, Judaism's most venerable prophecies and vastest hopes were coming to fruition.

The prophet Isaiah wrote:

Arise, Jerusalem, for your light has come, the glory of God has risen upon you. The nations shall come to your light and kings to the brightness of your dawning; the wealth of the nations is coming to you, convoys from the East, bringing gold and incense and singing the praise of the lord. (Isaiah 60:1,3,5-6)

The Adorction of the Magi by Gentile da Fabriano, 1420, with the gorgeous detail typical of the International Gothic style

The Magi see and worship Jesus in the star: from *The Bladelin Altarpiece* by Rogier van der Weyden, c. 1450

Herod I, King of Judea

Cruel, paranoid, and held in the grips of madness, Herod I ruled the ancient kingdom of Judea with an iron fist, brutally slaying any who opposed him

WRITTEN BY CHRIS FENTON

Herod of Idumea was born into one of the most volatile regions of the ancient world. He quickly learned to fear rivals, suspect betrayal, and watch his own back. The Romans had taken over much of his native land, and solidified their grip on the area through unpopular puppet kings. Rebellion was in the air, and from a young age Herod was forced to pick sides—work with the invaders or fight for an independent homeland. His father was a high-ranking official of King Hyrcanus II and had the ear of the Roman senate, so he used this prestigious position to grant Herod a governorship in 49 BCE in the province of Galilee. Herod knew this position came from powerful Roman patronage, and he made sure the Romans knew he would continue supporting them if they supported him by instigating a brutal regime in Galilee for the glory of Rome.

Unfortunately for Herod, not everyone shared his astute sense of accommodation when it came to the Romans. In 40 BCE, the puppet king Hyrcanus died and was replaced by Antigonus, who quickly set about ejecting the Roman garrisons from Judea and exterminating any of his subjects who had conspired with them against their own people. For Herod, this meant he lost his power and position. He was forced to flee into the night, and lacking anywhere else to go, he traveled to the heart of the Roman empire to beg Caesar to help him.

Herod's presence in Rome was not an unusual one; many high-ranking foreigners traveled to the sprawling city to seek patronage and aid from the Roman senators who decided the fate of kingdoms. What was unusual was how unpopular Herod was within the city. The Jewish population saw him as a tyrannical traitor and the Romans saw him as an incompetent beggar. The decision by the senate to make Herod King of the Jews was only made through a lack of a better option. As far as Caesar and the senators were concerned, Judea needed a leader who was strong and loyal to the Roman cause. Herod wasn't strong, nor was he particularly loyal, but he understood power and the protection Rome could offer him if he became their puppet.

With thousands of Roman legionaries behind him and one of Rome's greatest war heroes, Mark Antony, by his side, Herod marched proudly back to his homeland as a conqueror in 37 BCE. He would not be satisfied with a mere governorship this time; he wanted ultimate power. He decided to ignore the outlying provinces and concentrate his forces around Jerusalem with the approval of Antony. The siege lasted for 40 days. The defenders were desperate to hold onto their new-found freedom from Roman oppression, but in the end Herod breached the walls and thousands of bloodthirsty Roman warriors stormed the city. The devastation was horrendous; the Romans slaughtered men, women, and children, brutally slaying the people who dared defy Caesar's will. Herod was outraged; he wanted to subdue the population, not butcher them, and he knew all of Judea would never forget the Jewish blood spilled that day. His complaints to Antony fell

During his reign, Herod commissioned a number of building projects, including a huge temple in Jerusalem

> "The Jewish population saw him as a tyrannical traitor and the Romans saw him as an incompetent beggar"

Life in the Time of Herod

Roman Rule
The Middle East, which consisted of the Jewish and pagan kingdoms located around the coastline of the Mediterranean, was influenced and controlled by the Roman rulers through vassals and puppet kings. The Romans needed the kingdoms for their resources and to guard the eastern flank of the empire from the ever-present threat of the Persians.

Culture Shock
Herod's kingdom was made up of a number of different tribes that settled in the area or who were cast out of Persia over the previous three centuries. Contrasting cultures were active in the region, some adopting Judaism while others followed Roman, Greek, or other pagan traditions, creating deep social divides.

Fractured
Due to the fractious nature of Judean society, many areas within the kingdom that Herod ruled did not recognize him as a legitimate king. Herod himself had very little in the way of military muscle to keep the different communities in line, and often had to rely on his Roman patrons to subdue the population.

Political Games
Herod's position as a Roman vassal was not an easy one. Roman politics was going through a radical transformation during this period, which involved violent civil wars. Herod had to make sure he was backing the right man, or if he wasn't, change sides quickly to avoid being disposed of.

Rebel Groups
Due to the brutal repression under Herod through the Roman legions stationed in Judea, a number of rebel groups sprung up, bent on ending his reign of terror for good. These groups were forced to fight a guerrilla war, as they could not raise a standing army that could beat Caesar's legions. ∎

on deaf ears—as far as he was concerned, it was all in a day's work.

Antony left Herod in the smoldering ruins of his new kingdom with enough Roman guards to keep an eye on him. From now on, Herod would be taking his orders directly from Rome. Immediately, Herod self-styled himself as high ruler of what remained of Jerusalem and the rest of Judea. His subjects were less than convinced; his claim to the throne was based on little more than the Roman bodyguards he had surrounding him. As a way of trying to gain some respect after putting his own people to the sword, he married his second wife—a Hasmonean princess called Mariamne—in 32 BCE. Mariamne was from an old Judean family that could trace its origins back to the conquest of Alexander the Great, and Herod hoped the marriage would give his rule an amount of legitimacy.

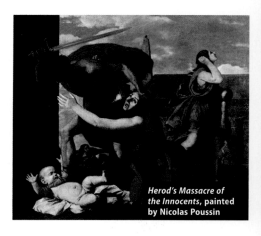

Herod's Massacre of the Innocents, painted by Nicolas Poussin

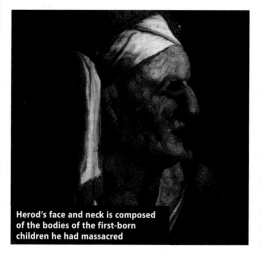

Herod's face and neck is composed of the bodies of the first-born children he had massacred

The marriage failed to gain the love of the people, and as he began to settle down to the task of ruling his unhappy kingdom, he felt more vulnerable. He feared assassination at every turn, particularly from his own family. He had his brother-in-law from his first marriage drowned in his own pleasure pool because he feared the Romans would prefer him as ruler of Judea. Then in 31 BCE, Herod received word that Rome had become engulfed in a power struggle between Octavian Caesar and Herod's old friend Antony. Like all vassals reliant on Rome's good will, Herod was forced to take sides, and in keeping with his preference for backing the strongest player, he chose Antony. The odds were very much stacked in Antony's favor, but he lost the struggle nonetheless, and Herod found himself in a very awkward position; the man in charge of Rome was the man he sided against. He sent a number of groveling letters to Octavian promising his undying loyalty in return for being allowed to keep his job as King of the Jews. Octavian reluctantly allowed him to remain king, again more through a lack of a better option than any reflection on Herod's skill as a leader.

Defining Moment
Fall of Jerusalem † 37 BCE
Herod, with the help of a number of Roman legions supplied by Mark Antony, invades Judea and lays siege to Jerusalem. The walls are surrounded and huge siege engines are built to devastate the city's populace hiding within the city. After 40 days of fighting, the townspeople begin to weaken through starvation, and Herod breaches the walls. When the Romans storm the city, they butcher the population. This angers Herod because his reputation would now be tarnished by the Romans' actions. Despite Herod's desire to appease the population after the siege, he still has the popular Antigonus executed because he represents a threat.

Timeline

74 BCE

● **Birth of Herod**
Herod is born in Idumea as the second son of Antipater—a high-ranking official in the kingdom of Judea. Antipater quickly maneuvers his son into a position of authority. **74 BCE**

● **Appointed Governor of Galilee**
Through his father's influence, Herod is made governor of Galilee—a Judean satellite state. His father continues to gain influence throughout Judea because of his good relations with the Romans. **49 BCE**

● **Flight to Rome**
After the anti-Roman king Antigonus II takes power in Judea, Herod is forced to flee and persuade the Romans to help him regain his power in the region. **40 BCE**

● **Elected King of the Jews**
During his stay in Rome, Herod convinces the senate that he should be made King of the Jews. The Romans agree with the proviso that he acts as a vassal on his return to Judea. **40 BCE**

● **Marriage to Mariamne**
Herod marries a Hasmonean princess, Mariamne, who is also a member of the Judean ruling class, in an effort to give his new status as King of the Jews legitimacy. **32 BCE**

Descent Into Madness

Despite having survived one of the most destructive civil wars in Rome's history, Herod remained uneasy. He became estranged from his wife after he had her placed under guard to prevent her from claiming the throne for the Hasmoneans if he died during the fighting. He heard more rumors of threats against his life, he feared Mariamne would try to grab power by killing him in revenge for having her arrested, his behavior became erratic, and he fell into a strange psychotic state of paranoia. While he was suffering from this break from reality, he became convinced Mariamne was going to kill him, so he acted. He had her beheaded, but as soon as the axe fell, he came around from

"After Agrippa left for Rome, Herod returned to the depths of paranoia"

his delusion and realized he'd made a terrible mistake. He wept uncontrollably for weeks and began hallucinating visions of his dead wife screaming in agony in the corridors of his palace.

In an effort to try and turn his mind away from these terrifying visions, he began to construct a grand temple designed to be the envy of the ancient world. Construction started just after the death of Mariamne, and was only halted briefly after a great famine struck. When Caesar's aide Marcus Agrippa visited the city in 15 BCE, he was amazed at the temple's construction and how modern Jerusalem looked since its sacking by Antony. Agrippa held court with Herod, and

Herod, knowing that weakness in front of the Romans could be dangerous, managed to hide his precarious mental state. Underneath this façade, he was edging ever closer to madness.

After Agrippa left for Rome, Herod quickly returned to the depths of paranoia. He slaughtered any who spoke out against his dictatorial regime, and the country lived in fear of his violent mood swings. He burned alive a group of rabbis and their students who had pulled down a Roman imperial eagle in a building in Jerusalem. He then executed two of his eldest sons because he thought they were plotting against him.

By 4 BCE, he feared that he had become so unpopular that no one would mourn his passing. In a fit of madness, he ordered the families of the nobility throughout the kingdom to attend him on pain of death. He then had them rounded up and placed under guard in the hippodrome. The guards were ordered to murder them when he died so his death would be mourned.

As the families in the hippodrome huddled together, terrified at the prospect of being put to death as a sacrifice to the passing of their own king, Herod laid on his deathbed racked with pain. He was suffering from kidney failure and the paranoid delusions that had finally left him senseless. He saw visions of his beloved Mariamne and was tortured by her mutilated face. When he finally died screaming in agony in 4 BCE, the holy men of Jerusalem proclaimed that his horrific death was, "the penalty that God was exacting of the king for his great impiety." Herod's sister countermanded the order to kill the Judean families and the kingdom celebrated; Herod 'the mad and wicked' was dead.

Massacre of the Innocents

Herod has been reviled in the Bible as the monstrous tyrant who threatened the life of the baby that Christians believe was the son of God. Jesus of Nazareth's birth came at the end of Herod's reign, when his psychotic episodes had become increasingly dangerous to the people he suspected were plotting treason against him. According to the Bible, it was during one of these paranoid episodes that he heard word of a child being born proclaimed as the "King of the Jews." This was highly threatening as far as Herod was concerned, as he had never been fully accepted by his Jewish subjects as their true king, and any kind of usurpation from another individual claiming to be their ruler had to be destroyed. He went into a fit of rage, ordering all the sons of Bethlehem, the birth place of Jesus, murdered in what became known as the 'Massacre of the Innocents.' While the Bible is not considered historically accurate by scholars, Herod's violent reaction was alluded to by Roman sources writing after the event, and archaeologists have speculated the massacre occurred at some point in 5 BCE, a year before Herod died. His actions have since been immortalized through the story of the Nativity, and his reputation for uncompromising brutality has never been forgotten in Christian traditions. ∎

Herod orders the execution of all first-born males in Bethlehem

Defining Moment
Trouble in Rome † 31 BCE
A Roman civil war threatens to engulf Judea in factional fighting and Herod must decide which man to support—Octavian Caesar or his old friend Mark Antony. Antony's force, stationed in Egypt, appears to be the strongest, and initially Herod sides with him. After Antony's defeat, Herod endears himself to Octavian, pledging his loyalty to the new Roman leader. While Octavian is unconvinced of Herod's honesty, he recognizes that he has served Rome well in the past, so allows Herod to stay on as King of Judea as long as he can control the population.

The Battle of Actium as depicted by Lorenzo A. Castro

Defining Moment
Death of Herod † 4 BCE
Herod dies in March or April 4 BCE after succumbing to 'Herod's evil', thought to be kidney disease and gangrene. He had already executed two of his eldest sons after another bout of paranoid madness, and he leaves Judea in open rebellion against Roman authority. The divided communities that make up the Judean state immediately demand independence, and only the presence of Roman legions under Octavian subdue the population adequately for Herod's three remaining sons to rule a third of the kingdom each under Roman patronage.

4 BCE

● **Mariamne Arrested**
In a fit of paranoia, Herod orders for Mariamne to be arrested after he fears that if he dies she will try and take the throne away from his son. This deeply offends Mariamne, and she becomes extremely hostile towards him. **31 BCE**

● **Death of a Princess**
After further rumors about a plot to poison him, Herod condemns Mariamne to death to prevent her from trying to seize power. This action haunts him for the rest of his life. **29 BCE**

● **Famine**
A great famine strikes Judea and its surrounding provinces. Herod is forced to halt some of his grand architectural projects in order to buy grain to feed the population. **25 BCE**

● **The Grand Temple**
As a way of appeasing the Jewish population, Herod builds a grand temple in Jerusalem. Little remains of the site today, but it was said to be one of the largest buildings in the entire city. **20 BCE**

● **Visit of Marcus Agrippa**
Agrippa visits the city to make sure Herod's loyalty has not abandoned him, and is astonished by the new masonry projects commissioned by the King of the Jews. **15 BCE**

● **Burning of the Teachers**
In one of Herod's most brutal acts, he orders the death of a group of rabbis who were found destroying a Roman eagle within Jerusalem. They are thrown in a pit and burned alive. **4 BCE**

Massacre of the Innocents

Artist: Pieter Bruegel the Elder

Year: 16th century

In a contemporary twist, Bruegel's scene recreates the Massacre of the Innocents in 16th-century Netherlands, with Spanish troops in lieu of Herod's brutal soldiers. Acquired by Holy Roman Emperor Rudolph II, he considered the scene too graphic and ordered that the slaughtered babies be overpainted with food or animals to make the scene less brutal. The scene was recreated numerous times by both the original artist and his son, Pieter Bruegel the Younger.

A Jewish Boy

The story of Jesus' unusual birth is the best-known part of his life. But what can we really say about his childhood?

WRITTEN BY EDOARDO ALBERT

In today's secular world, the most familiar image of Jesus is that of a baby in a crib, alongside his mother, father, angels, kings, and shepherds, together with a donkey, a cow, and sheep. It's the subject of school Nativity productions and plays a walk-on part, alongside Santa, at Christmas.

The Evidence for Jesus

But did it really happen like that? After all, what can we say about something that supposedly happened over 2,000 years ago? While emperors and generals were recorded in the histories written of the time, there's precious little recorded about the lives of ordinary people and, if Jesus existed, he certainly numbered among the ordinary people whom history forgets. But leaving aside the Gospels for the moment as biased sources, what other evidence is there for his existence?

Writing around 116 CE, the Roman historian Tacitus says in his account of the rumors circulating in Rome blaming the Emperor Nero for starting the Great Fire in 64 CE, that Nero had shifted the blame onto the 'Chrestians', a cult that followed one Christ who had been executed by the Roman official, Pontius Pilate, during the reign of Emperor Tiberius.

The Jewish historian, Josephus, writing under the patronage of the Roman emperors, also mentions Jesus, twice, in his work *Antiquities of the Jews* (published c. 93 CE). The second reference is to the execution of James, the "brother of Jesus who is called Messiah;" this is uncontroversial. The first reference, known as the Testimonium Flavianum, is longer and much more detailed, but has clearly had text interpolated by later Christian copyists.

However, taken with the second reference, it can be seen as solid non-Christian evidence for the existence of a Jewish teacher called Jesus. Indeed, working solely from Tacitus and Josephus, it's possible to say that Jesus existed and his name, in Aramaic, was Yeshua, of which Jesus is the Greek version; he was called by some the Messiah, or *Christos* in Greek; he had followers among Jews and Gentiles; he was opposed by Jewish leaders; and the Roman governor, Pilate, ordered his execution by crucifixion between 26 CE and 36 CE.

Apart from these two historians, Jesus is also mentioned by a number of other ancient writers, in contexts more or less pleasing to his followers. The 2nd-century satirist, Lucian of Samosata, mocked all belief in the supernatural, that of the Christians whom he satirizes in his work *The Passing of Peregrinus* no less than that of followers of traditional Roman religion. The mix of ideas that Lucian lampoons as typically Christian in his work suggests that he used other sources than the New Testament and Christian writings, most likely contemporary pagan appraisals of this relatively new cult. Celsus, a 2nd-century Platonist philosopher, argued that Jesus was a magician who had

The young Jesus debates a mob of scholars, or temple elders, when he remains at the temple in Jerusalem after his family leave

A photograph of the Church of the Nativity in Bethlehem, taken in the 19th century, when the population of the town was less than 4,000

An exotic view of what the Jewish historian, Josephus, would have looked like. In reality, he probably dressed as a high-status Roman

tricked people with his powers. Jesus and his followers are also mentioned in a letter written by Pliny the Younger to the Emperor Trajan around 112 CE, and in Suetonius' thoroughly scurrilous and hugely entertaining *On the Lives of the Caesars*.

It's also worth noting that no ancient author ever argued that Jesus did not actually exist. Even in the most heated arguments between Jewish and pagan writers and early Christians, neither the rabbinical nor the Classical authors suggest that Jesus was a mythical figure: whichever side of the argument they were on, there was agreement that they were talking about a man who had walked the dusty roads of 1st-century Judea until his crucifixion. It was only in the 19th century that the idea of Jesus as a mythical rather than a historical figure was seriously advanced, although few scholars now hold that idea seriously.

Taken together with the historical fact of the rise of a new religion that traced itself to Jesus, and the complementary but not coordinated writings of the New Testament,

most if not quite all scholars of the New Testament believe that the question of the historicity of Jesus has been answered definitively: yes, there was such a man.

Where was Jesus Born?

But while the question of the historicity of Jesus has been solved, there is little agreement over the well-known stories attached to his birth. The familiar narrative that we see reenacted, with varying degrees of cuteness in Nativity plays is a weaving together of two very different accounts of Jesus' birth given in the Gospels of Matthew and Luke. Jesus' birth and early life are simply not mentioned in the Gospels of Mark and John, and there are no other sources even vaguely contemporaneous to which we can turn (many further details, that have worked their way into the traditional Christmas story, actually come from the Christian apocrypha, most notably the Protoevangelium of James, which was written around 145 CE). Some scholars argue that Mark and John's

Gospels assume that Jesus was simply from Nazareth, with no mention of the idea that he might have been born in Bethlehem, far to the south (Bethlehem lies five miles south of Jerusalem, Nazareth roughly 65 miles north of Jerusalem, in a different Roman province). The reason for Matthew and Luke pulling Jesus from his home town and plonking his birth so far further south, they argue, is to establish him more firmly within the Jewish prophetic tradition; indeed, Matthew explicitly says at various points within his narrative that what happened to Jesus and his family was to fulfil "what the prophet has written." (Matthew 2:5) Similarly, Luke is concerned in his, quite different, account to situate Jesus within Judaic tradition. So, did the authors of these Gospels, knowing that the Jewish prophetic tradition required the Messiah to come from Bethlehem, manufacture their stories to match what they were convinced was true? Believing Jesus was the Messiah, he would have had to have been born in Bethlehem, and they therefore wrote it that way. So was Jesus really born in Nazareth, and are all those innocent Nativity plays simply reenacting a series of pious fabrications?

It isn't necessarily so. The criticism of the Nativity stories is mainly based on forensic examination of the differing accounts in Matthew and Luke, but usually either ignores or dismisses the archaeological evidence in favor of Bethlehem as the birthplace of Jesus. This evidence stands in the formidable shape of the Church of the Nativity in Bethlehem, its massive granite blocks rising over a cave and the 14-pointed silver star in the cave that is said

Bust of the Emperor Trajan, to whom Pliny the Younger wrote asking advice on how to deal with Christians

"The 14-pointed silver star in the cave in Bethlehem is said to mark the spot where Mary gave birth to Jesus"

A view of Nazareth taken in 1893, when its population was around 7,000 people

Home is Where the House is

In Nazareth, archaeologists have uncovered the carefully preserved remains of a house that was later venerated as the place where Jesus grew up with his family. The remains were found on the site of the Sisters of Nazareth Convent, across the road from the Church of the Annunciation that traditionally marks the place where Mary conceived Jesus. Archaeologists began examining the site in 2006, and swiftly found remains stretching back many centuries, including successive Byzantine and Crusader churches. But what was of greatest interest was the structure that the churches had been built to enclose, and had thus preserved. It was a courtyard house, cut from the limestone as it sloped towards the valley below it, and it could be securely dated to the 1st century through the datable pottery found within it. Fragments of limestone vessels suggest the people who lived here were Jewish, since limestone containers could not become impure and as such were very popular with the Jewish population. The surrounding churches had been carefully built to protect and preserve the building over which they were raised. In the 7th century, a pilgrim visitor to Nazareth, Adomnan, who had come all the way from Iona, described a church raised over the site of Jesus' childhood house, which was subsequently lost. Professor Ken Dark and his team have probably found it again, although we cannot say for certain whether those early church builders had identified the correct house. But what is certain is that Jesus, at the least, grew up in a house very much like this one. ∎

to mark the spot where Mary gave birth to Jesus. The tradition that this cave was where Jesus was born was well-established by the early 2nd century, for it is reported by Justin Martyr, himself a native of Palestine, that when Joseph could find no room at the inn, "he moved into a certain cave near the village, and while they were there Mary brought forth the Christ and placed him in a manger." But while local Christians maintained that the cave was the site of Jesus' birth in Justin Martyr's time and later, they could not themselves visit it. For Emperor Hadrian, as part of his devastating response to the Third Jewish Revolt from 132-136 CE, had erected a pagan citadel atop Temple Mount, and set about extirpating the practice of Judaism, and its daughter faith, Christianity, from the land of their birth. So from 135 CE until the reign of Constantine and the Edict of Milan in 313 CE allowing Christians

freedom of religion (a span of 178 years), the cave that local Christians stubbornly insisted was the site of the birth of their god was actually consecrated to the cult of Adonis and Aphrodite, and they would not have been permitted to worship at this pagan shrine. That the local people did not simply relocate the cave to somewhere more accessible suggests strongly that the tradition was so strongly established that they did not feel able to do so.

As far as the two Gospel sources go, Matthew and Luke are drawing from two completely independent sources: that both sources should agree on the place (Bethlehem) and the time (during the reign of Herod the Great) of Jesus' birth argues for their reliability. And while the early Church certainly did think of Jesus in terms of a fulfilment of Messianic prophecy, the Jewish idea of the Messiah—a warrior king of the line of David who would drive

A view of the excavated remains of a rock-hewn house in Nazareth that, archaeologists have discovered was built in the time of Jesus

A view of Nazareth today, with the Church of the Annunciation in the center of the picture, and a population in the greater Nazareth area of over 200,000

Portrait of the Roman historian and senator, Publius Cornelius Tacitus

Jesus partaking in what he almost
certainly spent much of his childhood
doing: learning his father's trade

Where Was Jesus?

From age 12 to about 30 we know very little of what
Jesus did or where he lived. The Gospels say nothing.
From such silence the religious imagination recoils,
and the various apocryphal Gospels and writings
spun tales to fill the gap. Later, as Arthurian romances
drew Joseph of Arimathea into their orbit, having him
bring the Holy Grail to Britain (which would become
the object of the greatest quest of the Knights of the
Round Table), it was but a short step to imagining
the young Jesus, apprenticed to Joseph, setting foot
in Albion—from which we receive the first verse of
William Blake's "Jerusalem." The 19th century saw a
number of scholars advance theories that the young
Jesus had traveled to the east and studied with a
varying cast of Hindu sadhus, Buddhist bhikkhus, or
Tibetan lamas. These ideas, although entertaining,
have nothing in the way of evidence. As Jesus
seems to have been known, before his ministry, as a
tekton—a general craftsman—like his father, there is
little reason to suppose he traveled any further than
Jerusalem. And as the signal achievement of modern
scholarship on Jesus has been to place him in his time
and place, a 1st-century Jew, there is every reason to
reject these theories. ■

A painting of Bethlehem from 1882 by Russian artist Vasily Polenov. Note the rural surroundings of the time

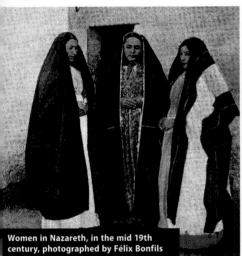
Women in Nazareth, in the mid 19th century, photographed by Félix Bonfils

Joseph, the tekton, turning his hands to one of the many jobs he would have undertaken in order to earn money for his family

out the foreign invaders and purge sinners and the unrighteous from Israel—was fundamentally at odds with the figure of Jesus: a man who was crushed by the political powers of his day and who, rather than purging the unrighteous and the sinful, sat down and ate with them. The early Church thought of Jesus as the fulfilment of the Davidic prophecies because of who they believed him to be and where he was born: Bethlehem.

Teen Dreams
Wherever Jesus was born, there is no doubt as to where he grew up: Nazareth. Although now Nazareth is a substantial town, in the 1st century it was little more than a village, home to maybe 400 people, situated on a ridge giving good views over the surrounding countryside. Much more significant, in terms of population and importance, was the town of Sepphoris, a cosmopolitan city deeply imbued with the Hellenistic culture of the eastern Mediterranean. However, Sepphoris had mostly been razed in Roman reprisals for Jewish disorder in the aftermath of Herod the Great's death in 4 BC. This was the time when, according to Matthew, Jesus and his family lived as refugees in Egypt. It was only when things stabilized under the reign of one of Herod's sons, Herod Antipas— whom Jesus would encounter later on the night of his trial—that the family returned to Nazareth.

"Jesus was intimately aware of ordinary people's struggles: he was one of them"

And there, in Nazareth, the story stops. We have one glimpse, from Luke, of Jesus and his family traveling to the temple in Jerusalem for Passover. According to Luke, they went every year to Jerusalem for the festival; after Jesus' birth, they had presented him there, with the customary sacrifice. But, being poor, they could only afford the lesser sacrifice of two pigeons, rather than a lamb.

Life in Nazareth was simple. Family life was communal and work was shared, whether that be drawing water from the well or grinding wheat under the millstone in the courtyard around which were set the homes of the family clan.

In Nazareth, Jesus' father Joseph likely found work helping with the rebuilding of Sepphoris, as well as doing local work. Jesus, as was expected of a poor Jewish boy of his time, would have learned his father's trade. Although that trade is usually translated as "carpenter," the translated word, *tekton*, has a wider meaning: Joseph was a general building and construction worker who could turn his hand to masonry and metal work as well. The nearest equivalent today might be the general handyman, willing to turn his labor on any job that needed doing and that would gain a day's wages: in poor countries today you

will still find, waiting at the market or by the bus station, day laborers hoping to be called for a few hours' work. Jesus knew such men well: they feature in one of his most memorable parables, that of the men called by the owner of a vineyard to work, some being called at dawn, and others at various points in the day, who all at the end of the day receive the same wage, to the expressed annoyance of those who had worked all day. Jesus, growing up, became intimately aware of the everyday life and struggles of ordinary people: he was one of them, and their stories help to give many of his teachings their unmistakably authentic pungency.

But while Jesus worked with his hands, sweating over his work, he was educated in the Jewish scriptures. Indeed, most of the Pharisees and rabbis of the day worked in a trade, thus gaining some measure of independence from the overweening power of the state. Indeed, Shemaiah, a Jewish scribe who lived a generation before Jesus, said, "Love labor and hate mastery and seek not acquaintance with the ruling power." Or, as rabbi Jacob Neusner put it, "Love work, hate authority, don't get friendly with the government."

The Finding of the Savior in the Temple
Artist: William Holman Hunt
Year: 1854-60

Unlike many artists who sought to recreate the familiar in their art, Holman Hunt was determined to paint an accurate scene of Christ among the doctors, visiting Jerusalem to use live models. Like Dürer's scene over 350 years before, Holman Hunt depicts Jesus's audience in a mix of emotions—some questioning, some appearing skeptical, and others angry.

"Preparing the Way of the Lord"
John the Baptist

How much do we really know about the man who helped set Jesus' ministry in motion?

WRITTEN BY JON WRIGHT

John the Baptist plays a starring role in Jesus' story (he is mentioned no fewer than 90 times in the New Testament), but concrete facts about his life are few and far between. In some of the Gospel narratives, he simply arrives upon the scene, already engaged in his ministry in rural Judaea. Other accounts offer a more substantial backstory. In Luke, John is described as the son of an aged priest, Zechariah (a descendant of Aaron) and his wife Elizabeth. The elderly couple hardly expected a child and John's birth is foretold by an angel. John will "drink neither wine nor strong drink and he will be filled with the Holy Spirit. (Luke 1:15) Elizabeth is portrayed (in just one Gospel) as a relation of Jesus's mother, Mary. The familial link is therefore tenuous, though this has not prevented artists through the ages seizing on the theme. Countless paintings depict the young Jesus and John together, often in tranquil domestic settings. All we can state with a high degree of probability is that John was born at some point in the final decade of the 1st century BCE.

Some scholars have made much of a single sentence from Luke: "He was in the wilderness until the day he publicly appeared in Israel." (Luke 1:80) It is suggested that this may hint at John's involvement with the rural Essene movement, often linked with the settlement at Qumran, though such ideas remain highly speculative (see boxout, overleaf). John emerges as a more fully formed character during his ministry, which had almost certainly begun by the third decade of the 1st century CE. He is seen living an ascetical life, wearing homespun camel-hair clothes, and feeding on locusts and wild honey.

The centerpiece of his mission is baptism by immersion in the River Jordan. The use of water in Jewish ablution rituals (the washing of hands and feet, for example) was common at the time, but John's dramatic practices are of a different stamp. Not for nothing is he described as "the baptizer." John sees the ritual as a process of repentance and purification. Salvation cannot be assumed simply because you are a descendant of Abraham; a transformative act is required. This is an urgent matter because, for John, a time of judgement is imminent. Before too long, the people of Israel will be winnowed like the wheat and chaff on the thresher's floor. The Jordan is the ideal setting for such endeavors; the river held great symbolic power, since God led his people across it on their way home from Egypt.

John's baptisms appear to have been very popular, drawing large crowds and many participants. The historian Flavius Josephus also stressed the ethical content

A 17th-century image, by Jan Steen, of John preaching in the wilderness

of John's message: he encouraged people "to practice virtue and act with justice toward one another." A radicalism is on display. Those on the margins of society (from tax-collectors to prostitutes) are not excluded, and John represents a deliberate separation from the Jewish establishment: he criticizes Pharisees and, in common with other baptizing movements of the time, his methods threaten to render the rituals of the Temple obsolete. At times, his words against the Pharisees and Sadducees are deeply provocative, likening them to snakes and warning that "the axe is already at the root of the trees and every tree that does not produce good fruit will be cut down and thrown into the fire." (Matthew 3:7-10)

Jesus and John

Jesus encounters John and proceeds to be baptized. The Holy Spirit descends on Jesus and a voice from above announces that "You are my son, the beloved; with you I am well pleased." (Mark 1:11) All along, John has been predicting the arrival of a figure greater than himself. John baptizes with water, but his successor will baptize with spirit and fire (fire is to be taken, here, in a symbolic sense). Is Jesus this man? In some of the Gospel accounts, John will come to express doubts: "Are you the one who is to come or shall we look for another?" (Matthew 11:3) In others, John recognizes Jesus as the promised messiah immediately.

In any event, the Gospels make great efforts to position John as Jesus's forerunner. He is sometimes portrayed as an equivalent of the prophets of Hebrew Scriptures. Perhaps he is the new Elijah (who also had a penchant for hair clothes) who would precede the arrival of the messiah. In Matthew, Jesus explicitly compares John and Elijah, though in John's Gospel, John the Baptist rejects the comparison. A parallel with the prophet Isaiah is also developed. There is a shared wilderness setting and linguistic echoes from the earlier text: talk of washing people clean from sin, and of the corrupt land of Israel being like a brood of vipers. A verse such as "I will send my messenger" (Malachi 3:1) cannot help but ring in the reader's ears.

"The Gospels make great efforts to position John as Jesus's forerunner"

The encounter with John is crucial in triggering Jesus's own ministry and, throughout, Jesus is very much a fan: "among those born of women none is greater than John." (Luke 7:28) Historians differ, however, over whether we should see Jesus, in these months and years, as a follower of John. He begins to baptize and it has been suggested that, at least for a short while, the two worked closely together. It also appears that some of John's supporters were among the first to rally to Jesus's cause. The Gospels only specifically mention Andrew in this regard, but additional links appear in the Acts of the Apostles.

Whatever the case, Jesus soon develops a ministry of his own, leaving behind the baptisms and concentrating on healing, exorcizing, and preaching. His deeds are as much about changing the here and now as about preparing for the future. Some striking differences emerge: Jesus concentrates on urban areas, and he and his followers do not adopt a particularly ascetic approach (they are more than happy to have full bellies). Continuities persist, however—not least themes of repentance and cleansing.

As for John, difficult times lie ahead. Herod Agrippa, tetrarch of Galilee and Perea, develops a hatred for John. In the biblical accounts, this stems from John's criticism of Herod's marriage to his brother's former wife—a clear violation of rules set out in Leviticus. In Matthew, Herod is eager to strike at John. In other Gospels, Herod is hesitant, because he recognizes John as a holy man, and requires some convincing.

This is supplied by his wife's daughter (often referred to as Salome) who dances for Herod and entices him into granting any wish she desires. In Flavius Josephus, more political motives are stressed. Herod feared that John's "great persuasiveness with the people might lead to some kind of strife (for they seemed as if they would do everything

John and the Essenes?

The Essenes were an ascetical, rather secretive Jewish sect that had emerged in the 2nd century BCE and cast off the authority of the Temple authorities in Jerusalem. They established one of their communities at Qumran, the site where the Dead Sea Scrolls were discovered in the mid-20th century. On the face of things, there are striking similarities between the Essenes and some aspects of John's message. Ritual washing, for instance, was a key part of their devotional regimen and they may have followed a rigorous diet. John, the voice in the wilderness, also seems to chime in with the idea, explained in one of the Qumran texts, that the righteous will "separate from the perverse minority . . . and go to the wilderness, there to clear the way of the Lord." John's baptisms in the Jordan took place quite close to Qumran and, with something of a stretch, it has been pointed out that since John reputedly had very elderly parents who could well have died during his youth, he may have required a safe harbor. Against this, John patently does not seek to separate himself entirely from the world; he is all about engaging with the people of Judaea. Some of the Qumran texts refer to John as a "unique teacher," but the lack of any clinching evidence makes the link between John and the Essenes a matter of pure supposition. ∎

Qumran Caves, where the Dead Sea Scrolls were discovered

John was held up as an exemplar of rigorous Christianity in the early Church. Here, Filippo Lippi shows him alongside St. Jerome, another, later advocate of asceticism

which he counselled)." Josephus adds that the crowds attracted to John were "aroused to the highest degree by his sermons," so Herod "decided that it would be much better to strike first and be rid of him before his work led to an uprising." In a longer, Slavonic version of Josephus's work, John ("in countenance like a savage") declares that "God hath sent me to show you the way of the law, by which you shall be freed from many tyrants."

John's Demise

Historians disagree about the nature of John's radicalism, though it seems unlikely that he was proposing outright revolt. Nonetheless, Herod was determined to snuff out any threat. His rule did not extend to Judaea (which was under direct Roman control), but as soon as John crossed to the far bank of the River Jordan, he could be

arrested. And so it transpired. John was taken to the fortress at Machaerus and decapitated. His head, famously presented to Salome on a silver plate, was beyond the reach of John's supporters, but they are said to have secured and buried John's body. His remains would enjoy a long and winding journey through posterity (see boxout, right).

Josephus records a hostile reaction to news of John's execution within the Jewish community. When Herod suffered military defeats shortly afterwards, "to some of the Jews the destruction of Herod's army seemed to be divine vengeance, and certainly a just vengeance, for his treatment of John." After his death, John would emerge as an interesting figure across various faith traditions. Some historians have suggested that, later in the 1st century CE, tensions developed between those who followed the teachings of Jesus and those who took John as a model.

those who took John as a model. This is highly speculative and we lack convincing evidence of a "baptizing" sect. Similarly, links between John's legacy and Gnosticism are difficult to establish during the Church's first centuries.

It is true, however, that one group—the Mandaeans—later adopted John as a figure of great significance. The Mandaeans subscribed to a dualistic view of the cosmos, in which the forces of light and darkness competed and in which the fleshly world was a prison to be escaped. Far beyond the theological mainstream, the Mandaeans were based in lands that form parts of modern-day Iran and Iraq and, during the 7th century, they were faced with Islamic invasions. In order to qualify as what Muslims termed a "people of the book," and to secure toleration, it was necessary to identify a central text and a prophet at the heart of their faith. They chose John the Baptist. He was a fitting figure, since baptismal rites were at the heart of the Mandaeans' devotions. It was

Caravaggio depicts Salome with the head of John the Baptist in a painting from c1610

John as a chi d in a painting
by Bartolome Murillo

Losing Your Head: John's Journey Through History

In common with so many figures from Christian history, the fate of John the Baptist's remains developed into something of an enigma. Tradition holds that his body was moved to Sebaste in Samaria. Here, his tomb became the focus of devotion and the site of miracles. During the reign of Julian the Apostate (in the early 360s), the tomb was despoiled and the contents scattered. Claims to possess parts of John's body have multiplied ever since, and cover an impressive geographical area. The Coptic Christians have always been particularly keen to make their case; as recently as 1978, new discoveries were reputedly made during restoration of St. Macarius monastery in Egypt. The story of John's head is even more confusing. Amiens Cathedral in France, the church of San Silvestro in Rome, and the Umayyad Mosque in Damascus have all been suggested as the home of this most precious of relics. John's remains continue to provoke speculation. In 2010, a knucklebone was discovered at a monastery on the Black Sea island of Sveti Ivan. Carbon dating and DNA testing showed that the artifact came from the 1st century CE. Nothing, of course, could be proven about precisely whose bone it was, but the island did enjoy trading links with Antioch which, up to the 10th century, was reputedly home to one of John's arms. ■

A shrine in Aachen Cathedral, said to contain the cloth on which John's severed head was placed

Abraham Janssen's portrayal of Jesus, John, and Mary together—a common subject in Western painting

an astute choice since John, like Jesus, was regarded by Muslims as being among the ranks of true prophets and messengers.

It is sometimes argued that John was recruited, even hijacked, by mainstream Christianity in order to provide a satisfying, coherent narrative. He was a convenient vehicle for invoking prophecies from the Hebrew Scriptures and to highlight God's greater plan. Even if this were true, there is no questioning the genuine devotion that has been afforded John through the centuries. Few figures have been more influential in the development of Christian thought or the outpourings of Christian art. In Mark's Gospel, John is referred to as the beginning of the good news of Christ and, in Acts, one of the hallmarks of the true apostle is that a person must have been there from the start, which is identified as Jesus's baptism in the Jordan.

It is striking that, in the early Church, John was also held up as a model of asceticism, and inspired the early eremites

and the first flowerings of monasticism. Some theologians attempted to portray John as even more rigorous than the Gospel texts suggested. The notion that he ate locusts was replaced with an image of John accompanying his wild honey with twigs and branches. This, so Isidore of Pelusium argued in the 4th century, showed how John "demonstrated exceeding suffering, not in poverty only, but also in ruggedness, by embittering every yearning of the body." In the same era, St. Jerome offered advice to a woman living in the sordid, grasping world of Rome. John was situated as the ideal role model.

After all, "he who eats locusts and wild honey cannot seek wealth or other worldly delights, but rather a strict and harsh life." It was wise to emulate John when surrounded by those "who are clothed in purple and linen and silk and seek soft things." It was a thought that resonated, with varying degrees of popularity, through the Christian centuries.

© WIKI

The Baptism of Jesus

This defining moment in Jesus' life marked the start of his ministry and inspired people to follow him in his total acceptance to the will of God

WRITTEN BY CHARLIE EVANS

The baptism of Jesus is widely recognized as the most important event of his life. Until this point, he had just been a carpenter. But Jesus' baptism would identify him as the son of God. It also marked the beginning of his ministry.

The story has became a pillar of Christianity, symbolizing spiritual purification and the cleansing of sin. It's chronicled by three of the synoptic Gospels (Matthew, Mark, and Luke), as they tell the account in parallel with each narrative describing Jesus as journeying from Nazareth in Galilee to John the Baptist by the Jordan River. John is described as a fearless and bold preacher characterized as no "reed shaken by the wind." (Luke 7:24) He directly addressed the sin of humanity and made a stand against the Pharisees. His message was one of moral reform to prepare the people for the coming of Christ. John quickly drew an audience of people from around Jerusalem and Judea who wanted to be baptized by him.

The Baptism

When Jesus was about 30 years old, John had been preaching for six months. He had been speaking to crowds of people about morality and forgiveness, offering baptism to cleanse themselves spiritually of sin. The Gospels depict John's initial hesitancy to baptize Jesus when he arrived at the River. He believed it should be Christ who performs the ritual cleansing, greeting him by saying, "I need to be baptized by you, and do you come to me?" (Matthew 3:14). But Jesus insisted, replying, "Let it be so now; it is proper for us to do this to fulfill all righteousness." (Matthew 3:15) The testament describes John consenting and laying Jesus into the river to be fully immersed by the water. When he was bought back up again, it's said that the Spirit of God descended like a dove and a holy voice proclaimed: "This is my Son, whom I love; with him I am well pleased." (Matthew 3:17)

Variation with the Scripture

There is little disparity between each of the Gospels in their account of the baptism of Jesus. The only notable distinctions being Matthew uniquely describing the holy voice addressing the crowd, rather than Jesus himself, and solely Luke asserting John as a relative of Jesus (Luke 1:36). Luke also describes the Holy Spirit descending in the bodily form of a dove in discordance with the metaphorical stance of the other three Gospels, which describe the spirit descending like a dove; "and the Holy Spirit descended on him in bodily form like a dove." (Luke 3:22)

Significance of Jesus' Baptism

Jesus' baptism at first glance may seem incongruous. Jesus was sinless and therefore didn't require repentance. It is a theme that runs through both the Old and New Testament—that he had "never sinned, and he never told a lie." (1 Peter 2:22) This is why John was confounded that the will of God was for him to baptize the Messiah rather than the contrary. But the point was never that Jesus required the rite to cleanse himself, but instead the doctrine illustrated both men submitting to God's will as an applauded act of obedience and piety. It is described best by St. Ambrose, a bishop of Milan in the 4th century, who wrote: "Our Lord was baptized because He wished, not to be cleansed, but to cleanse the waters, that, being purified by the flesh of Christ that knew no sin, they might have the virtue of baptism." (St. Ambrose, quoted in Aquinas' Summa Theologiae, III, Q 39, Art 1)

Jesus' baptism showed that he humbled himself to identify with man, but also gave John the opportunity to demonstrate to his own followers that Jesus was the redeemer for which they had been waiting. John the Baptist is recognized as the forerunner of the Prophet, and had long claimed there was a King coming. He preached the word of Messianic hope, calling for people to repent in preparation for the coming of Jesus (Isaiah 40:3) and claiming that "the one who is coming after me is stronger than I am, and I am not worthy to carry his sandals." (Matthew 3:11) Jesus coming to John for his baptism showed his endorsement of John's work, and it confirmed that his message was recognized by God. It would prove to be important later when John's authority was questioned, particularly after his arrest by Herod (Matthew 14:3–11).

His baptism also revealed Jesus' identity as the son of God as he instituted a new sacrament for his followers to succeed. Just as modern baptism today remains a form of recognizing those who follow Christ, people who received baptism from John were also identifying themselves—they were the ones who had faith that the savior would come to them. The practice of baptism in the Christian faith remains across many denominations as a sign of a sign of repentance and faith. However, Christian baptisms today differ slightly in meaning in that the rite is one of fulfillment rather than expectation.

Where was Jesus Actually Baptized?

The baptism of Jesus is viewed by most modern scholars as one of the Bible stories for which a high level of certainty can be ascertained. However there is some contention about the exact location of the Biblical event. The Jordan River extends through the Jordan Rift Valley and flows into the Dead Sea but theologians struggle to pinpoint which side of the bank the baptism took place. Matthew and Mark both describe Jesus coming from Galilee to the Jordan River near the wilderness to be baptized by John (Matthew 3:13, Mark 1:9) but the Gospel of John expresses a slightly different description of the location as "Bethany beyond the Jordan." (John 1: 28) Not to be confused with the village Bethany east of Jerusalem, John is referring to Bethabara in Perea on the Eastern bank of the Jordan River, near Jericho. The unattested location in the scripture, coupled with the conflicting information from 1st-century historians, means today two sites battle for recognition as the real location of Jesus' baptism. The narrow Jordan River serves as an international border with the Al-Maghtas site laying on the east bank in Jordan, and its counterpart, the Yardenit site sitting on western bank in Israel. Because Al-Maghtas is the oldest historically observed location, and includes the remains of an ancient monastery, churches, and baptism ponds, it remains recognized as the official location of Jesus' baptism. ∎

Pope John Paul II looks over the Jordan River, where Jesus' baptism is thought to have occured

The Temptation of Jesus

Satan attempted to lead Jesus from his path of morality by coaxing him with alluring sins—but Jesus' strength in the face of temptation is a teaching opportunity in ethics and integrity

WRITTEN BY CHARLIE EVANS

This illustration of Jesus and Satan on a mountaintop in the wilderness was published in Bible or Books of New Testament or Old Testament, 1875

Following his baptism, "Jesus being full of the Holy Ghost returned from Jordan, and was led by the Spirit into the wilderness." (Luke 4:1-3) His time spent in the desert was intended as preparation for his imminent mission, as he focuses his mind by denying himself food and spending time praying to God. But here he was tempted by Satan. The event is only omitted by the Gospels of John, and describes Jesus' time fasting for 40 days and 40 nights (Luke 4:2) in the harsh Judean Desert. It was at the end of this time of solitude living amongst nature and without food that Satan is said to have approached Jesus and tried to tempt him three times, appealing to the allures of hedonism, egoism, and materialism. Jesus battles the Devil by reciting Old Testament scripture. When Jesus does not succumb, Satan leaves the wilderness and Jesus returns to Galilee to start his ministry.

The Story of the Temptation

While the Gospel of Mark only offers a brief summary of the event, it is chronicled in further detail by Matthew and Luke. Here, the minutiae of the conversations between Jesus and Satan can be read. Both Gospels lend detail to the temptations offered by Satan: making bread from the stones in the wilderness so he can eat to relieve his hunger; jump from a pinnacle and call on the angels to break his fall; and to worship the Devil in return for all the kingdoms of the world. In response to Satan's command to turn the stones into bread, Jesus stands strong by his integrity in the face of hunger and responds quoting the scripture (Deuteronomy 8:3) "One does not live by bread alone, but by every word that proceeds from the mouth of God." (Matthew 4:4) The tempter also takes Jesus to the Holy City, which is considered by most Christians to be Jerusalem, and to the pinnacle of a temple and tells him to prove he is the son of God by throwing himself from the top so that angels may come and save him. Once more, Jesus patiently responds by quoting scripture, this time (Deuteronomy 6:16), saying, "Again it is written, 'You shall not put the Lord, your God, to the test'." (Matthew 4:7) The Devil's final temptation is to ask Jesus to give up the control he has over all of the kingdoms of the world (Ephesians 2:2) in return to form an allegiance with Jesus. Matthew describes the Devil taking Jesus to a high mountain where all the kingdoms of the world can be seen; "All this I will give you,"

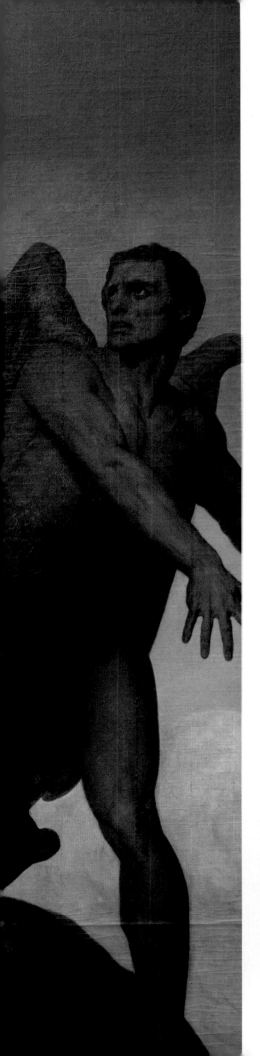

he said, "if you will bow down and worship me." (Matthew 4:8-9) Jesus again retorts with scripture (Deuteronomy 6:13), "Away from me, Satan! For it is written: 'Worship the Lord your God, and serve him only'." (Matthew 4:10) Traditionally, this summit that Jesus was tempted upon is recognized to be Quarantania, a limestone peak that towers approximately 366 meters over the town of Jericho in the West Bank. With disturbing foreshadowing, "He departed from Him until an opportune time," (Luke 4:13) suggesting it is not the only battle that Christ will face against the Devil, and that he will return again. After Satan has left Jesus, who is now weak with hunger and exhaustion, Mark and Matthew both describe angels descending to tend to Jesus.

A Parable or a Literal Event?

The Biblical story can be understood either as a parable emanating from Jesus' want to communicate his inner experience to his followers, or as an account of an autobiographical event. It is a subject that has caused much discussion amongst scholars around the world. The view that the account of the temptation is a parable comes from the conclusion that it was told with the purpose of illustrating a spiritual lesson. It seeks to highlight the conflict between God and Satan as well as the foundational downfalls of the human condition; though God incarnate, Jesus was also bodily human and felt the same starvation we would feel if we went such a time without meals. The writings of the temptation show that the Devil will attempt to take advantage of human weakness, and that followers can recognize and combat the temptations through scripture. Jesus affirms his commitment to God's will down to his last word.

This first temptation was an attempt to entice Jesus to use the powers for his mission for his own gratification. The order in which Satan presents the temptations differs between Gospel, suggesting they are not necessarily listed chronologically, but that the importance lies within Christ's triumph at each point, rather than the order in which

he faced them. It is possible that this is due to the intent being to make a profound theological point rather than tell an accurate account of the event. Fasting continues across many faiths as a symbolic religious practice that demonstrates the believer's commitment to strengthen their faith, and increases their humility through denying themselves physical needs to focus on their repentance and connection with God.

Regardless of interpretation, whether the temptation is seen as a description of a factual event or a parable, the verses continue to serve as a reminder of how Jesus responded to temptation, and the faithful can follow in his footsteps in the face of such adversity.

Artist Briton Riviere's *The Temptation in the Wilderness* shows Jesus alone in contemplative thought

The Devil and Temptation

Satan is represented in the Bible as a fallen angel who once served by God's side, but rebelled against him and fell from Heaven. He is known by other names (Devil, Lucifer, Antichrist) but the common theme is where God is good, Satan is evil. The testaments of the Bible describe various accounts of Satan tempting people. He enters the heart of disciple Judas Iscariot and tempts him to betray Jesus (John 13:2), and leads Ananias astray by tempting him to lie to the Holy Ghost about keeping money (Acts 5:3). The tension and interactions between God and Satan show the constant battle between good and evil. People who choose to sin are seen as those who have chosen to be on the side of the Devil: "The one who does what is sinful is of the Devil, because the Devil has been sinning from the beginning. The reason the Son of God appeared was to destroy the Devil's work." (1 John 3:8) ■

Satan is depicted sitting in Hell in a 1879 engraving

© Alamy, Getty

The Twelve

A teacher with Jesus' charisma attracted supporters from the earliest days of his ministry, but his specially chosen Apostles would be the men to witness his most dramatic moments and carry forward his teachings

WRITTEN BY JON WRIGHT

Christ and the Apostles break bread during the Last Supper

From among his many disciples, Jesus chose a group of men to form what might be thought of as his inner circle. They came to be known as the Apostles. On one level, their role was to act as companions and share in Jesus' travels and travails. But they would also contribute to the evolution of Jesus' ministry and the spreading of his message after the resurrection and ascension. The portrayal of the Apostles is not consistent across the four Gospels, but common themes emerge. They are there to witness Jesus's deeds, to question him, and to be his students— learning lessons about humility, God's purpose, and the need to care for others.

At times, the Apostles are granted opportunities for independent action; Jesus sends them out into the community to heal, pray, and exorcise demons. All along, however, they seem to represent the essence of Jesus's encounter with humanity. The choice of Apostles is often significant. The first four to be chosen—the brothers Peter and Andrew, and the brothers James and John—are all fishermen. They pull up their nets and abandon the security of their profession to follow Jesus and become fishers of men: an act of sacrifice. Matthew, another early recruit, was most likely a tax collector and, as such, a member of a detested profession. Jesus incurs criticism for associating with such a man, but his selection of Matthew seems to demonstrate that the Christian message is open to all sectors of society. After Jesus has shared a feast with Matthew, the Pharisees ask, "Why do you eat and drink with sinners?" to which Jesus bluntly replies: "It is not the healthy who need a doctor, but the sick. I have not come to call the righteous, but sinners, to repentance." (Luke 5:30-2)

The Human Touch

One of the most compelling aspects of the Gospel narrative, clearly visible in Mark (the most plain-spoken of the Gospels), is the tension between Jesus's understanding of his mission and how this is interpreted by his disciples. The fierce commitment of his followers is always stressed, but their incomprehension or confusion sometimes bubbles to the surface. In Mark, the disciples seem unable to grasp the significance of Jesus feeding the 5,000 from a few loaves and fishes. They are perturbed when Jesus walks on water, and positively shocked when he manages to calm a storm on the Sea of Galilee. "They were terrified and asked each other, 'Who is this? Even the wind and the waves obey him'," which earns a swift rebuke from Jesus: "Why are you so afraid? Do you still have no faith?" (Mark 4:39-41) When Jesus predicts his bloody demise, Peter cannot quite understand how this could happen to a putative Messiah, and when Jesus talks of the new kingdom to come, James and John brashly ask, with a clear sense of ambition, if they will enjoy lofty roles there, seated on his left and right hand. In Mark, Jesus gives vent to his frustration, talking of men with eyes that do not see and ears that do not hear.

None of this diverts the trajectory of the Apostles' role. They are there to learn and to bring the Gospel narrative to fruition. Even their worst moments allow the plot to unfold. Three Apostles fall asleep while

Jesus is praying in Gethsemane, and when Jesus is arrested they flee; Peter denies Jesus three times; Judas betrays Jesus to the Sanhedrin. A sense of grim necessity hangs over all these events.

Perhaps the best way to understand the portrayal of the Apostles is through a prism of preparation. Crucial as they are to Jesus's ministry during his lifetime, they will come into their own following Jesus's death. The Gospels, and subsequent New Testament texts, hammer home this point. The Apostles enjoy unique eyewitness status and are best placed to recount Jesus's deeds and teachings, and to testify to his resurrection and ascension. As Peter puts it, they are "men who have accompanied us during all the time that Lord Jesus went in and out among us, beginning from the baptism by John until the day when he was taken up from us." (Acts 1:21-2)

This is no small task. Following the resurrection, Jesus spends 40 days instructing the Apostles, but he had also promised, at the Last Supper, that the Holy Spirit would descend upon them. This, in the Gospel account, is precisely what happens at Pentecost. The Apostles are able to speak in the languages of many different peoples—Parthians and Egyptians, people from Libya and Mesopotamia—and no less than 3,000 converts are secured. An excellent start,

and this launches the Apostles' most urgent mission: to spread the Christian message to, as Jesus demanded, all nations. Here, the literal meaning of the word Apostle—one who is "sent out"—comes to the fore.

Quite how subsequent events unfolded is difficult to verify. In Acts, mention is made of some specific missions: we hear a great deal about Peter's travels, for instance, and Philip heads to Samaria. Most of the other tales of the Apostles' odysseys derive from legend and non-Biblical sources, though the supposed geographical reach—throughout the Mediterranean, down into Africa, and even as far as India—is certainly impressive. We also know little for certain about most of the Apostles' ultimate fates. Only the death of James is recorded in the New Testament, though tradition holds that all of his fellow Apostles, with the exception of John, met bloody ends at the hands of persecutors. Various methods of crucifixion, defenestration, and the deployment of spears, stones, and arrows all feature in the gruesome accounts.

Similar uncertainty hangs over the question of the Apostles' remains and, through the centuries, many places have claimed to possess the genuine relics of Jesus's closest associates. The emperor Constantine famously hatched plans to build a basilica in which he could be entombed,

surrounded by containers holding the relics of all Twelve Apostles. This proved to be an impossible task, not least because the precise whereabouts of such precious artifacts was always a hotly contested issue. Some Apostles have endured long and winding posthumous trajectories: Andrew is said to have died and been buried at Patras, Greece, but his supposed remains were transferred to Constantinople during the 4th century, and seized by Italians and shipped to Amalfi during the 13th century. Relics associated with St. Thomas can still be found from Chennai in India to Ortona in Italy. John Calvin, always keen to poke fun at the devotions of Roman Catholicism, marveled at those Apostles who, what with all the relics, appeared to "possess two or three bodies."

The quest for the genuine resting places of these important figures continues and, with striking regularity, some archaeological enterprise or the other will claim to have discovered the burial place of an Apostle or a locale associated with an Apostle's life. Not so long ago, much excitement was generated by the unearthing of a tomb in Hierapolis, Turkey, which some believed to have once housed the remains of the Apostle Philip. The site of Julias, formerly Bethsaida, and the hometown of Peter, Andrew and Philip may recently have been

The leading Apostle, Peter, denies Jesus in this work by Gerard Seghers

A medieval book of hours shows the rogue Apostle, Judas Iscariot, kissing Jesus and setting the events leading to the crucifixion in motion

The Seventy Apostles

In Luke (though not mentioned in the other three Gospels), Jesus instructs 70 of his followers to go out "to every city and place whither he himself was about to come" because "the harvest is indeed abundant, but the workmen few." (Luke 10:1-4) In the western Christian tradition, these 70 are referred to as disciples, but the Eastern Orthodox Church names them as Apostles. They are each celebrated at different times during the liturgical calendar, and all together on January 4. In the early Church, various lists of the 70 (sometimes 72) emerged but, in all versions, these Apostles are an impressive bunch. They include Jesus' brother, James; Ananias, who baptized Paul; Stephen, the first martyr; and Paul's companion Barnabas. Many of the early bishops of places such as Milan, Alexandria, Corinth, and Ephesus are included, and names familiar from Acts also make notable appearances. As with the Twelve Apostles, cruel deaths await some of the Seventy, but the talents displayed by some of the Apostles are impressive: Agabus has the gift of prophecy, while the mere shadow of another Apostle is able to heal the sick. We even encounter a Roman senator, Pudens, who is said to have provided lodging for Peter and Paul during their fateful sojourn in the Eternal City. ∎

A Greek manuscript shows the Seventy Apostles gathered together

The Apostles gather around Christ at the Last Supper, depicted here by Pascal Dagnan-Bouveret

Additional Apostles

In the wake of Judas's betrayal and death, a replacement was required. Following Jesus's ascension, the Apostles assembled and cast lots to choose between the two leading candidates, Joseph and Matthias. Matthias won the day. Little more is known of his deeds from the Biblical record, but tradition holds that he traveled around Greece, then on to the Caspian Sea and Georgia. Opinions differ regarding the place of his death. In the 4th century, his tomb was allegedly discovered in Jerusalem and his remains were transferred to Trier, Germany. Others claim that he was buried in Georgia. In Acts, we gain a firm sense of the apostolic torch being passed from the original Twelve to worthy successors like Barnabas and Stephen, who would become Christianity's first martyr. St. Paul also comes to the fore and he would go to great lengths to claim the mantle of Apostle for himself. This was accepted within the New Testament texts and seems appropriate for the man who, through his many journeys across the Mediterranean, did more than any other to spread and define the early Christian Church. ∎

St Matthias, the Apostle who replaced Judas

Jesus bids a final farewell to his Apostles

"The quest for the genuine resting places of these important figures continues"

discovered. Even the fate of the grandest Apostle of them all, Peter, remains a matter of debate and conjecture. In the 1930s, workmen in Rome discovered a necropolis containing a tomb whose inscriptions indicated that Peter had been buried within. The papacy, by the 1960s, had firmly declared that this proved that Peter had assuredly perished in the city. Some historians, however, remain unconvinced.

After Jesus

The central text for assessing the activities of the Apostles after Jesus' ascension is Acts, in which important themes emerge. The Apostles' status as Jesus' privileged representatives is signaled by their ability to perform miracles of their own: Peter heals a lame beggar, cures someone who has been bed-ridden for eight years, and, at Joppa, raises Tabitha from the dead. Angels also appear to be on the side of the Apostles, rescuing them from incarceration on more than one occasion. Peter, who often strikes the reader as the senior Apostle in the Gospels, moves even closer to center stage in Acts. At Pentecost, skeptics suggest that the Apostles' babbling in strange tongues might be the result of drinking too much wine. Peter, in one of his many crucial speeches, assures the crowd that divine inspiration is the true

explanation. Peter also leads the charge in the work of bringing Jesus' message to the Gentiles—notably through his encounter, in Corinth, with Cornelius the centurion. At the council of Jerusalem, Peter adjudicates over decisions about whether Gentile converts should be required to undergo circumcision.

Here, indeed, was a prime example of how the Apostles could shape the future contours of the Church. In Antioch, arguments had simmered about the status of Gentile converts to Christianity. Was a non-circumcised person entitled to fully embrace the new faith? The well-traveled Paul and Barnabas returned to Jerusalem to seek an adjudication and, at the council, held in or around 48 CE, it fell to Peter to announce the momentous decision. God, he explained, "gave the Holy Spirit to the Gentiles exactly as he did to us." (Acts 15:8) Idol worship remained forbidden, and dietary rules still had to be followed, but circumcision would not be required of Gentile Christians. In one stroke, this boosted Christianity's chances of becoming a truly universal religion (rather than a Jewish sect) but also created bitter tensions within the ranks of Christianity's Jewish converts.

Ultimately, the Biblical accounts of the Apostles will always be our primary source of information, because evidence

from elsewhere is decidedly scarce. The expansive corpus of apocryphal texts that bear the names of Apostles only adds to the confusion. This naturally makes any investigation into them problematic.

Difficulties crop up at the simple level of identifying who was who. The Early Church historian Eusebius declared that "the names of our savior's Apostles are sufficiently obvious to everyone," but this was a rather optimistic assessment. The names of most Apostles are consistent across the four Gospels, but others shift from text to text. In Matthew, Mark, and Luke, we meet Bartholomew, but in John this Apostle is referred to as Nathaniel. Jude in John becomes Judas "son of James" in Luke, Thaddaeus in Mark, and Lebbaeus "whose surname was Thaddaeus" in Matthew. Just as frustratingly, a number of figures receive hardly any significant mentions beyond inclusion in lists of the Apostles. So, while it is possible to learn a great deal about Peter, James, and John (who appear to have enjoyed special status), we know close to nothing about the likes of Simon the Zealot or Philip. There is no particular reason to suppose that the individuals represented in the Gospels were anything other than genuine historical figures, but they will always remain, in many important ways, enigmatic.

Ten of the Twelve Apostles are reputed to have met bloody ends. Here, we see the martyrdom of Andrew

Les Très Riches Heures du Duc de Berry depicts the Apostles going forth to preach

The basilica at Santiago de Compostela, the supposed resting place of the Apostle James

Meet the Twelve Apostles

1
Peter
The man dubbed by Jesus as the "rock of my church," Peter (referred to as Simon in the Gospels of Matthew and Luke) famously denied Jesus three times but is often thought of as the chief of the Apostles. Tradition holds that he founded the churches at Antioch and Rome.

2
Andrew
Like his brother Peter, Andrew was a fisherman from Bethsaida. He is identified in John's Gospel as a disciple of John the Baptist. He is said to have traveled as far as Kiev and Byzantium, where some say he suffered martyrdom. Other legends take him as far afield as Scotland.

3
James
James, along with his brother John, was the son of the fisherman Zebedee. The two were referred to as the "sons of thunder," indicating that, while calm by nature, they could be prompted to anger. Acts relates that James was executed by Herod. His remains are reputedly at Santiago de Compostela.

4
John
One of only a few witnesses to various pivotal events in the Gospel narrative, including the raising of the daughter of Jairus, John is often identified as being particularly beloved by Jesus. He is traditionally held to be the Apostle seated directly next to Jesus at the Last Supper.

5
Philip
One of the more obscure Apostles, though he was present at the wedding at Cana, Philip is thought to have had a telling impact on evangelical efforts in Greece and Syria. He enjoys a major presence in non-canonical texts and serves in the role of patron saint of hatters.

6
Bartholomew
Another Apostle who left few traces in the New Testament texts, Bartholomew (named as Nathaniel in John's Gospel) was believed by some to have traveled as a missionary as far as Ethiopia, Mesopotamia, and India. He is often shown enduring a gruesome death— being skinned alive.

This fresco in the Vatican depicts Jesus calling Peter and Andrew from their nets

7
Thomas
Thomas famously doubted Christ's resurrection, insisting that he would only believe it if he saw the holes in Jesus's hands made by the nails and the spear wound in Jesus's side. The supposed travels of Thomas to India, allegedly to the region of Kerala, are a matter of scholarly debate.

8
Matthew
Matthew is most often described as a tax collector, a much-despised profession in Jesus's society. Less well-traveled after Jesus's death than many of the Apostles, Matthew was held, from the 2nd century, to be the author of Matthew's Gospel, though this issue continues to provoke much argument.

9
James, son of Alphaeus
Also referred to as James the Less (distinguishing him from James, the brother of John), this Apostle receives only four mentions in the Gospels. He is said to have been crucified in Egypt and some have, rather unconvincingly, equated him with Jesus' brother James.

10
Jude
The saint of lost causes in the Roman Catholic tradition, Jude's destinations after Jesus's ascension are said to include Mesopotamia, Armenia, and Libya, and he is reputed to have been killed with an axe in Beirut.

11
Simon the Zealot
Also referred to as Simon the Canaanite, he is the Apostle who makes the least significant appearances in the Gospels, only being mentioned in lists of Jesus's chosen followers. For all that, many places compete for the honor of being the site of his martyrdom.

12
Judas Iscariot
The man who betrayed Jesus to the Sanhedrin for 30 pieces of silver. He died, by one account, by hanging himself and, by another, "all his bowels gushed out." His role in provoking Jesus's death was, however, crucial to the fulfilment of the Gospel narrative, and he receives considerable praise in some Gnostic texts.

The Calling of Saint Matthew

Artist: Caravaggio

Year: 1600

Remembered today for his brawls, gambling, and even murder, in his day Caravaggio was one of the church's favorite artists—even Pope Francis declared this artwork a must-see. Perhaps reminiscent of Caravaggio's own less-than-savory background, Matthew is depicted with several other men counting money, while Jesus and Peter to the right of the scene beckon Matthew. Which of these immoral men is Matthew, however, is ambiguous—some suggest the man hunched over coins is Matthew, while others argue that the pointing man is indicating toward himself.

Mary Magdalene

The prostitute-turned-Apostle to the Apostles is an enduring icon of Western civilization, but we know surprisingly little about who she really was

WRITTEN BY ROBIN GRIFFITH-JONES

Early on Easter morning, when it was still dark, Mary Magdalene came to Jesus' tomb. She knew where it was. By Jesus' death, all his male disciples except one had abandoned him. It was the women—his mother, Mary Magdalene, and others—who watched his agony to its very end. They saw his hurried burial too, in a tomb (cut into a quarry), the entrance of which was then closed with a rock.

Now here is Mary Magdalene, after the Sabbath, back at the tomb. She has brought ointment with her to clean Jesus' body. It is John's distinctive version of the story that we hear. The tomb is in a garden. Mary comes alone. She finds the rock pushed away from the entrance and the tomb itself empty. She goes to tell two of Jesus' principal disciples, Simon Peter and the anonymous "disciple whom Jesus loved." They come back with her, confirm her story, and leave. There is something almost dull about these men.

Mary, far from leaving, is crying inconsolably. She looks once more into the tomb and sees two angels in white. She turns away and there in the garden is Jesus. She fails to recognize him; she thinks he is the gardener. "Woman," he asks, "why are you crying? Who are you looking for?" She wants only to know where Jesus' body has been put, so she can take it away. Now Jesus addresses her by name: "Mary." She recognizes him and tries to touch or cling to him but he doesn't let her. "Go to my brothers and tell them that I am ascending to my father and your father, to my God and your God."

Robin Griffith-Jones

Robin Griffith-Jones is Master of the Temple at the Temple Church, London, senior lecturer at King's College London, and author of Mary Magdalene: The Woman Jesus Loved.

This is a wonderful Bible story, extraordinarily intimate, at first achingly sad and then, even in its triumph, a scene of poignant renunciation. Mary Magdalene is given the supreme privilege. She is the first to see the risen Jesus on Easter Day and is commissioned to spread the incredible news. No wonder Mary Magdalene came to be called the Apostle to the Apostles in later centuries.

We are bound to wonder why was she so privileged? Who was she as a person, and indeed what was she to Jesus, that he appeared first to her? In our own time, speculation has run wild. Surely, we read in *The Da Vinci Code*, she was married to Jesus or they were lovers. 50 years ago, it would have been scandalous to admit how sensuous John's story becomes when he reaches Easter morning. It poses the question whether any other stories tell of Jesus and Mary in such terms.

Defining Moment

Independent Woman

Mary was among the women who provided for Jesus and his followers as they traveled though Galilee. All these women had been healed by Jesus. According to Luke 8.2, seven devils had gone out of Mary herself. Mary must have been a strikingly independent woman, especially for the time. "Magdalene" may refer not to a home-town of Magdala or "tower" but to her being a tower of strength.

Defining Moment

Death of Jesus

When Jesus was arrested, almost all of the men in his entourage ran away. It was chiefly the women who stayed to see Jesus crucified outside Jerusalem's western gate. Such executions were deliberately cruel and public. Mary Magdalene was among the women and so was Jesus' mother—they were no threat to the executioners. Here, Mary Magdalene became a silent heroine.

"This is a wonderful story, extraordinary intimate, at first achingly sad and then, even in its triumph, a scene of poignant renunciation"

Mary Magdalene and Scandalous Behavior

It is hard to know. Though it is widely accepted that Magdalene was a real historic figure, there are very few sources about her. A whole biography of Mary has been spun from almost nothing. She was allegedly a prostitute who came to Jesus to ask for or acknowledge his forgiveness, who knelt before him, washed his feet with her tears, dried them with her hair and then anointed them with perfumed oil. This is another startlingly sensual scene. No wonder Jesus' host was scandalized.

Once assured of Jesus' forgiveness, she became one of the women who traveled Galilee with Jesus and provided for him out of their own means. Our Christian

Mary at prayer is often eroticized

ancestors will have believed more about this Mary Magdalene. If we combine all the four Gospels' distinct narratives into one story, Jesus is anointed not once but three times. First by the prostitute, then by his friend Mary, the sister of Martha and Lazarus. Martha was the more active, Mary the more contemplative of the two sisters. They begged Jesus to help their brother Lazarus who had died, and Jesus—in his climactic miracle— raised Lazarus from the dead. This Mary then anointed Jesus' feet with hugely expensive perfume, in anticipation, said Jesus himself, of his own burial. And finally, just a few days later, an anonymous woman anointed not Jesus' feet, but his head.

This is an odd series of overlapping stories. At the end of the 6th century, Pope Gregory the Great tried to bring all their ambiguities to an end. All these stories, he insisted, involved just one woman: Mary Magdalene, the penitent prostitute. First, she had wept over Jesus' feet in sorrow and regret; then she had anointed his feet again in honor of his impending death; and then she was considered worthy enough to anoint his head. No wonder she came to the tomb on

Easter Day with a jar of ointment, ready to anoint him yet again. But the buried body was not there and she is granted an incomparably greater honor in the first sight of the risen Lord.

This Mary Magdalene was no longer just an individual in Jesus' entourage. She had become a symbol of all Christians, men and women alike: sinful, penitent, forgiven, restored, and finally to be blessed with the sight of Jesus himself. And so she remained in Christian teaching and imagination for over 1,000 years.

However, there were flaws in this story. The penitent prostitute in Luke's Gospel is anonymous— Luke does not link her with the Mary Magdalene whom he introduces in his next scene. There is no reason to identify Mary Magdalene with Mary the sister of Martha and Lazarus; 'Mary' was simply a common name, shared by Jesus' own mother and at least two of his friends. The Mary Magdalene of the Christian Middle Ages is dissolving before our eyes. This Mary, woven out of the four Gospels' different narratives, may have provided a moving story of divine grace and human restoration but it seems to have been very bad history indeed.

Defining Moment

Witnessing the Rise

Early on what we now know as Easter Sunday, Mary saw the risen Jesus. According to John's Gospel, she was alone and had gone to anoint him with oil—the privilege was entirely hers. John has shaped the whole scene, while the other Gospels tell of several women and differ on their sight of Jesus. John's Mary and Jesus will apparently meet in the new Eden of a new-born world. It was Mary who told of Jesus' resurrection.

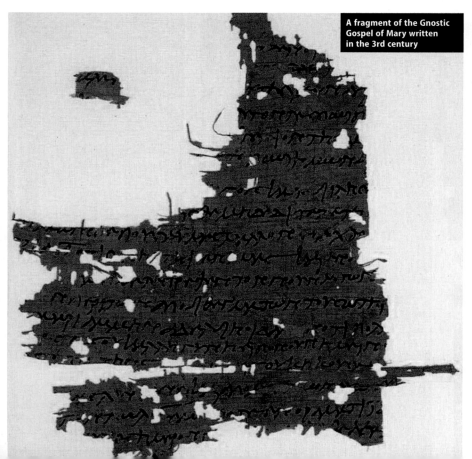
A fragment of the Gnostic Gospel of Mary written in the 3rd century

Mary Magdalene is often depicted covered in hair as she used her locks to dry Jesus' feet

Jesus backs away from Mary Magdalene

"She had become a symbol of all Christians, men and women alike: sinful, penitent, forgiven, restored, and finally to be blessed"

We should probably go further. That story of human fall and restoration is inspiring but it also portrayed the paradigmatic sinner as a woman whose sin was sexual. In churches dominated all through the Middle Ages by celibate men, this reinforced a terrible stereotype: that the most dangerous of all temptations lay in a woman's sexual power. Churches, tending towards misogyny, found fuel for their fear and anger. One need not be a revolutionary to be glad that the Medieval Magdalene has been left behind. In 1969, the Roman Catholic Church acknowledged that the Marys and the anointing women should no longer be celebrated as a single woman.

A Disciple Favored Above All Others

Where does this leave Mary Magdalene herself? Within a century of Jesus' death, there were groups on the fringes of the principal churches who saw in Mary a heroine of insight and faith, and she was the leader favored above all others by Jesus after his resurrection. It may well have been the admiration of women's leadership, in Jesus' day and in their own, which led to the suppression of these so-called Gnostics and their texts.

For such Gnostics, Mary represented the human soul, always seen as feminine, yearning for union with her spiritual Lord. This was intense and intimate but as often as not involved, for those Gnostics who hated the squalour of the physical world, a resolute renunciation of any sexual contact on earth. The rediscovery of this privileged Magdalene, so long lost from view, has become an icon of religious women's liberation in our own time from centuries of misogynistic patriarchy.

The Gnostics' Mary Magdalene was largely created out of John's Easter story. Spiritual tradition states that we too should end where we began, with the mysterious poetry of that Easter scene. John's whole Gospel is a story

> ### Defining Moment
> **Favored Disciple**
> Gnostic Christians of the 2nd and 3rd centuries saw Mary as the recipient of Jesus' deepest and most secret teaching. She was, for them, a leader and teacher that the male disciples—and even their successors, who ran the churches—could never be. These Gnostics' texts were suppressed and lost for nearly 2,000 years, before their rediscovery at Nag Hammadi in Egypt in the 1940s.

of the new creation. In Genesis, God created light on Day One, "completed" creation on Day Six, and put Adam in the Garden of Eden to be its gardener and to name all God's other creatures. Adam is finally given Eve as his companion. According to John's Gospel, Jesus "completes" his work at Day Six (Good Friday). On Day One (Easter Sunday) of the next week, Mary comes to the tomb before the light rises.

She mistakes Jesus for the gardener, but he calls her by her name, revealing his true identity.

Despite deep-rooted misogyny, a series of women has punctuated John's story: Jesus' mother at beginning and end, Mary and Martha right at the center. Mary Magdalene is the last and appears in the greatest of these scenes—she is the reader of John's Gospel, invited back as a new Eve into the Garden of Eden to meet the Jesus who far transcends any Adam. The 'new creation' is complete. The light is rising in paradise.

Today a Roman Catholic chapel sits on the mount at the historically recognized location of the Sermon

The Sermon on the Mount

Jesus' famous Sermon continues to be one of the greatest pieces of moral discourse in historical literature and ties together the heart of his entire message into one piece of discourse

WRITTEN BY CHARLIE EVANS

The Sermon on the Mount is told exclusively in the Gospel of Matthew. It is one of the longest speeches to have been given by Jesus, and is chronicled in three chapters in Matthew (5-7). They talk of Jesus climbing a mountain to give his messages and, if adhered to, results in being blessed in life and rewarded in heaven. At this time in his life, Jesus had been traveling and preaching, teaching in synagogues and tending to the sick. His message and actions continued to make local authorities uncomfortable, but he was admired by everyday people. He had gained a great number of followers from throughout Jerusalem, Judea, and Galilee. The Bible explains that to speak to the great assembly of people, he climbed up a mountain to speak to them: "Now when Jesus saw the crowds, he went up on a mountainside and sat down. His disciples came to him, and he began to teach them." (Matthew 5:1-2)

Jesus is recorded in the Gospels as having began his Sermon with The Blessed Attitudes: blessings focused on important moral values including love, kindness, and humility. The blessings, known as the beatitudes, read as a set of moral guidelines. Jesus' Sermon goes on to advise on how Christians should be living their lives, saying that they should "Love your enemies and pray for those who persecute you" (Matthew 5:43) and "Do not judge, so that you may not be judged." (Matthew 7:1) The collection of sayings and teachings from Christ also include the Lord's Prayer, and he also importantly highlights the move from traditional good acts such as alms (Matthew 6:1-4), prayer (Matthew 6:5-15), and fasting (Matthew 6:16-18), instead asking followers to focus on being good from their hearts rather than carrying out these activities for recognition.

An 1860 wood engraving by Julius Schnorr von Carolsfeld depicting Jesus' Sermon on the Mount

"Jesus' Sermon remains as important today to modern Christianity as it was in its own time"

Throughout the Sermon Jesus seeks to establish the new covenant. He's building on points that Moses has already made in his speech of the Ten Commandments, but improving each moral point and making it more specific. He tells his followers that he knows they follow the Old Testament teaching but he wants them to take each more seriously and more extended. He does this by repeating, "You have heard [Old Testament]. But I tell you [new covenant]." This can be seen particularly clear when Jesus reiterates the commandment not to murder—"You have heard . . . 'You shall not murder . . . But I tell you that anyone who is angry with a brother or sister will be subject to judgment." (Matthew 5:21-2) The piece of prose is so fundamental to Christian societies that many of the everyday phrases we use today come directly from the Sermon on the Mount, including 'turn the other cheek' (Matthew 5:38) and "Blessed are the meek, for they will inherit the earth." (Matthew 5:5)

The Location of the Sermon on the Mount

The location of the Sermon is generally thought to be on the Mount of Beatitudes which is on the northwestern shore of the Sea of Galilee, also known as the Lake of Gennesaret, in Israel. However, the Horns of Hattin, an extinct volcano in Lower Galilee, has also been suggested by some as the true location. The exact location is shrouded in controversy, and scholars have yet to reach a consensus because the Bible only describes the Sermon as taking place somewhere on a mountain between the Lake of Gennesaret and the fishing town Capernaum that is positioned on the northern bank of the lake.

In the 4th century CE, a church was built near the Mount of Beatitudes. Although only remains survive today, the Byzantine structure continues to mark the place historically associated with the location of the Sermon.

The Significance of the Sermon

The Sermon is not only a direct teaching of moral guidance, but it set, for the first time, the terms of the New Covenant of God by promising eternal divine blessings to his audience of those who obeyed and believed in his message; "Whoever does and teaches them [the commandments], he shall be called great in the kingdom of heaven." (Matthew 5:19) The principles Jesus addressed on the mount formed the basis of today's Christianity. It was the first time that the new covenant had been laid out concisely and directly to the masses. Jesus sought to convert the believers into true disciples by inspiring them to commit to the eight beatitudes within their lives. Jesus' Sermon remains as important today to modern Christianity as it was in its own time.

Two Similar Sermons

An interesting comparison can be drawn between the Sermon on the Mount and the Sermon on the Plain which can be found in the Gospel of Luke (6:17-49). Scholars are divided on the subject, with some of the belief that these were two separate sermons at different occasions and are unrelated, while some believe that they are just different accounts of the same event. They have similar teachings and beatitudes but the Sermon on the Plain includes a set of four woes that do not appear in the Sermon on the Mount.

The Q Source

It is accepted that the Gospel of St. Mark is the oldest of the books, and that the other Gospel writers, including both Matthew and Luke, have resourced this original text. Theological scholars expect that this conjugation is responsible for creating passages in both that are considerably similar to one another. Both books also contain common passages that are not found in the other Gospels, leading scholars to believe that their origin can be traced to an earlier source that has been lost or destroyed through the ages. This source is known as 'Q' (from the German Quelle, meaning 'source') and was first hypothesised before 1900. It can be used as an explanation for similar recurring patterns throughout the Bible that seem to be drawing from a common source. This leads to the belief that the Sermon on the Mount and the Sermon on the Plain are not two stories representing distinct historical events but rather crafted slightly differently to establish a different theological message in each story. The predominant differences being in whether Jesus ascended or descended to speak to man; "he came down with them [the Twelve], and stood in the plain" (Luke 6:17) conveying God coming down to humanity to speak with mankind versus "seeing the multitudes, [Jesus] went up into a mountain" (Matthew 5:1) as a symbolic action of power. ∎

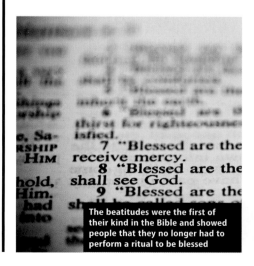

The beatitudes were the first of their kind in the Bible and showed people that they no longer had to perform a ritual to be blessed

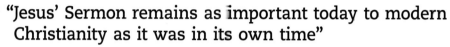

Miracles and Ministry

Jesus deployed many tactics to help spread his message: from preaching and parables to the performance of spectacular miracles. What was he trying to convey, and how did the Jewish authorities respond?

WRITTEN BY JON WRIGHT

Miracles were one of the pulse-beats of Jesus' ministry, from the early days in Galilee up to the climacteric in Jerusalem. These miracles can be neatly divided into broad categories. The Gospels provide accounts of a half-dozen major exorcisms in which demons are cast out. For the most part, Jesus follows conventional methods and the hapless victims of possession display typical symptoms: from the gnashing of teeth to feats of extraordinary strength. At times, though, the ill-tempered demons appear to recognize Jesus' special status: one of them even refers to him as "Son of the most high God." (Mark 5:7)

Healing is another recurrent theme and all manner of ailments are tackled: paralysis, deafness, dropsy, leprosy, blindness, and various other complaints. More spectacular yet are the handful of occasions when Jesus is reported to have brought people back from the dead. Finally, we encounter the miracles where Jesus seems to be able to break the normal rules of nature. These include turning water into wine, walking on the Sea of Galilee, calming turbulent seas, and cursing a fig tree so that it withers away.

These stories contain many layers of meaning and carry various consequences. At the most basic level, performing miraculous tasks wins Jesus support. Peter, John, and James are convinced to become disciples after Jesus appears to produce an unusually bountiful haul of fish. Following a healing at the synagogue, it seems as if the "whole city" (Mark 1:33) is eager to encounter Jesus. It is worth noting, though, that Jesus fluctuates between courting attention and keeping his miraculous exploits secret. He asks one healed leper not to spread word of his recovery and he deliberately takes the blind man of Bethsaida outside of the town and requests that he tell no one what has transpired. By contrast, after Jesus casts demons into pigs, the man who has been exorcised asks if he can follow Jesus but is told to remain where he is and relate his inspiring tale.

For the Gospel writers, the miracles amply demonstrate Jesus' special abilities. As one leper puts it, "if you choose, you can make me clean," (Mark 1:40) but Jesus is often at pains to stress that an individual's belief is truly responsible for his or her recovery: "your faith has made you well." (Mark 5:27) The specific words used to describe Jesus' interventions encapsulate (when literally translated) the different ways of looking at these events: "deeds of power," "signs," "remarkable things," or simply "doing good."

More is at stake than spectacle. Deeper meaning is easily located in the miracle stories. When Jesus calms the waters on the Sea of Galilee to save the boat in which he and his disciples are traveling, it is tempting to see the boat as a symbol of what will one day become the Christian Church. When Peter is allowed to catch all those fish, this prefigures all the souls he will help to save as a fisher of men. Jesus' message, meanwhile, is open to all, so who better to have falling to his knees and pleading for assistance than the wealthy and influential

A medieval illuminated manuscript depicts one of Jesus' most famous miracles: walking on the waters of the Sea of Galilee. Peter, to the right, attempts to emulate the feat, but he will be unsuccessful

The story of the wise and foolish virgins, here depicted by Hieronymus Francken, was one of the most popular parables among medieval and early-modern religious artists

Jairus, whose daughter is in peril? The miracles also provide links to the past and the traditions of Hebrew Scripture. When Jesus feeds the 5,000 from a few fish and loaves of bread, he is caring for his people in a way that recalls Moses; he is the shepherd to his sheep, feeding his people as Moses did in the wilderness. Hints of the future can also be glimpsed. The crowds mock Jesus ahead of the miracle of Jairus' daughter, just as they will mock him again.

One of the hallmarks of Jesus' miracles is that he never asks for any reward, though this hardly insulated him from criticism. The Pharisees are sometimes infuriated by Jesus' actions. When the son of an official at Capernaum is healed, Jesus announces that the boy's sins are also forgiven. The Pharisees grumble that Jesus is in no position to dispense such an adjudication: "who but God alone can forgive sins?" (Mark 2:7) The miracle of the man with the withered hand takes place in the synagogue, on the Sabbath, and this leads to a heated debate about what exertions are permitted on the Holy Day. Immediately afterwards, the Pharisees begin plotting Jesus' downfall. The raising of Lazarus, and the stir it provokes, leads to similar misgivings.

The miracles divide opinion. Jesus' followers take them as a marker of divine approval, but the Pharisees suspect the involvement of "Beelzebul, the prince of demons." (Matthew 3:22) Future Christians would see the miracles as proof of Jesus'

"The Jesus of the Gospels is a master of the pithy one-liner, and he imparts his wisdom through aphorisms"

status as the Messiah, but Christianity's critics would level charges of sorcery. The 2nd-century Greek philosopher Celsus, who had many unpleasant things to say about Jesus and the fledgling Christian Church, determined that "it was by magic that he was able to do the miracles which he appears to have done."

For the modern reader, the miracles are perhaps the most challenging aspect of the Gospel narrative. Responses have ranged from taking the events literally, to reading them allegorically, to seeking non-supernatural explanations of what may have happened. It's noteworthy, too, that even the Gospel writers varied in their approaches to reporting Jesus' miraculous exploits. Not all the miracles are in every text; versions of the stories can vary in their details, and while the Gospel of Mark is full of these tales (they make up almost a third of the verses), the Gospel of John adopts a much more cautious approach. Exorcisms are avoided and stories that do not appear elsewhere (such as the turning of water into wine at the wedding in Cana) come to the fore. The fourth Gospel seems to hone in on miracles that highlight Jesus' divine identity: one of the chief goals of its author. The reader is informed, without any hint of ambiguity, that miracle stories are being

recounted "so that you may come to believe that Jesus is the Messiah, the Son of God." (John 20:31)

Parables and Preaching

Miracles were the most dramatic aspect of Jesus' ministry. Throughout his travels across Galilee, Perea, Judea, and in the final stages in Jerusalem, Jesus relied on words as much as deeds. He preached and debated at synagogues, in the open air, in both public and private settings, to large crowds or small groups. Sometimes the courtyards of the Jerusalem Temple played host to his musings; sometimes he simply chatted over dinner.

The Jesus of the Gospels is a master of the pithy one-liner, and he imparts much of his wisdom through aphorisms. Parables are every bit as important. The genre has many advantages: Jesus' parables are short, their basic meaning can usually be grasped without too much mental exertion (though some are more cryptic than others), and they rely on imagery and settings that would have been familiar to a 1st century audience. The parables conjure up a world of baking bread, sowing crops, and the chores and challenges of everyday family life. As with the miracles, these famous stories are put to different purposes here and develop coherent

In addition to feats of miraculous healing, the Gospels also tell of revivals from death or near-death. In this medieval woodcut, Jairus's daughter is the recipient of Jesus' ministrations

A Bible Full of Miracles

Miracles make numerous appearances in what Christians refer to as the Old Testament. Many of them bear striking resemblances to the feats that were performed by Jesus. Elijah, for example, raises a widow's son, just as Jesus will bring back the child of the widow of Nain. Tellingly, Jesus' deed prompts someone to comment that "a great prophet has arisen amongst us." (Luke 7:16) This helps to solidify the links and parallels between Jesus and the prophets of the Hebrew Scriptures. Perhaps the greatest wonder-worker of the Old Testament is Elisha. At various times he makes poisoned food wholesome, makes an axe float on water, and increases the store of a widow's oil. Again, some of Elisha's miracles are reminiscent of Jesus' later marvels. He multiplies 20 loaves so that 100 people can be fed (much like Jesus' intervention at the wedding of Cana) and he cures Naaman of leprosy. Elisha, just like Elijah and Jesus, is also shown to have the ability to raise the dead. When a woman loses her son, she first tries to revive him by laying the corpse on Elisha's bed, hoping that contact with possessions of the prophet will suffice. When this fails, she seeks out Elijah in person and he dutifully performs the requisite miracle. ∎

A Dutch stained glass window from the 16th century depicts the prophet Elijah's raising of a widow's son from the Old Testament

themes across the Gospels. However, once again, the fourth Gospel is set apart from the others: allegorical language is much preferred to parable in John.

One of the recurrent tropes is that a great undertaking (in this case the flowering of faith and the establishment of the kingdom of God) often develops from humble beginnings. We see this in the Parable of the Sower. He casts his seeds in a haphazard manner: some land on the path, or on rocky ground, or on earth chocked by thorns, and only a few find their way to good, rich soil. Jesus' message, as the parable suggests, is rather like that, too. Many will reject it, but those who embrace the truth will be richly rewarded, just like the plant that emerges from the fertile corner of the field. The Parable of the Mustard Seed makes a similar point. At the outset, all we have is the tiniest of seeds but, given time and nourishment, it will develop into a plant taller than the tallest herb. Likewise, the Parable of the Leaven: add a little yeast to your flour the night before, and by morning you will have the makings of a delicious, fluffy loaf.

Jesus was, when necessary, perfectly capable of engaging in sophisticated theological debate but, in the parables, fundamental matters of faith are boiled down to their essentials. God's love extends to the most isolated person which is why, in the Parable of the Prodigal Son, even the loyal son who stayed at home should rejoice at his brother's return. As the Parable of the

Lost Sheep insists, when one animal out of 100 goes missing the dutiful shepherd leaves the other 99 to search for the sheep that has slipped away.

Not that everything can be left up to the shepherd. The pious person has a responsibility to behave in an ethical way. He should follow the example of the Good Samaritan who, despite his people's ancient rivalries with the Jews, proves to be a good neighbor and helps the man injured by the roadside. Jesus' followers must learn the importance of forgiveness and, as one parable suggests, emulate the rich man who does not pursue money owed by his servant. This is far preferable to following the example of the self-same servant who refuses to forgive a much smaller debt.

Devotion, the parables explain, is not always easy. Persistence is often required and so, when engaging in the delicate task of prayer, you should think of the man who comes home late at night and asks his neighbor for something to eat. At first, the neighbor refuses, but eventually he relents. If you hope to fare well on the day of judgement, preparation is everything. Best, then, to take heed of the Parable of the Ten Virgins: five of them are ready for the arrival of the bridegroom and are rewarded, but the five who fail to prepare themselves are disowned. You should not, as the Parable of the Great Banquet indicates, turn up for a wedding feast in unsuitable clothing: you are likely to be ejected. In the end, as the

Parable of the Tares announces, we will all be on one or other side of the great divide: some will be the righteous wheat but others will be the wretched weeds.

The Message

As homely and entertaining as the parables might seem, Jesus expected his audiences to take them very seriously. As the Parable of the Wise and Foolish Builders explains, those who accept Jesus' teachings are like

Rembrandt's take on the Parable of the Prodigal Son: a tale of forgiveness and redemption

the man who erects his house on rock, making it impervious to rain, wind, or flood. Those who dismiss Jesus' vision are like the man who builds his house on sand, only to see it collapse. The use of parables was not, in and of itself, a novel technique (it had long played a role in the dispensing of rabbinic wisdom), but Jesus' methods, as reported in the Gospels, broke new ground. He often poses a question, but provides no straightforward answer: the listener or reader is left with work to do. He also overturns expectations. In the Parable of the Workers in the Vineyard, an employer pays a full day's wages to those who have only labored for an hour, and those who have toiled from morning to night are dismayed. The reader may well share their outrage, but Jesus is making the point that human and divine perspectives are different: God's love and rewards are boundless.

The parables epitomize the peaceable character of Jesus' ministry. He was not one of those 1st-century firebrands calling for revolution, and he offers no specific commentary on contemporary political events. He resorts to violence only once: during the Cleansing of the Temple. The essence of his message is found in the Sermon of the Mount, with its beatitudes and pointers towards the value of love and humility. The meek will inherit the earth, the persecuted will be rewarded, and blessings will come to those who hunger for righteousness and remain pure in heart.

This should not distract us from the underlying radicalism of Jesus' message. He frequently speaks of the concept of God's Kingdom. Frustratingly, Jesus' precise understanding of this idea is never articulated (though that may be part of the point) but it is clearly not as simple as the removal of Roman rule from Palestine or some dramatic apocalypse. It is perhaps best understood, not as a geographically limited 'place', but as an event in which the presence of God will permeate a world characterized by peace and beneficence. If Jesus is the Messiah, this is what he heralds.

Jesus' Key Miracles

● **Water Into Wine**
Jesus and his disciples are invited to a wedding feast at Cana. Supplies of wine run out but Jesus saves the day by transforming more than 100 gallons of water into wine.

● **The Official's Son at Capernaum**
A royal official comes to Jesus asking him to cure his ailing son. Jesus does not need to attend the patient in person (he is some miles away) and simply announces that all will be well.

● **The Miraculous Haul of Fish**
Jesus is by the shore of the Sea of Galilee and encourages fishermen to make one last catch. The results are spectacular and the incident helps convince Peter, Paul, and James to become disciples.

● **The Man with the Withered Hand**
This healing in a synagogue provokes debate about whether such activities ought to be undertaken on the Sabbath. Jesus points out that if your sheep fell down a hole on the Sabbath you would surely rescue it.

● **Calming the Sea of Galilee**
Jesus and the disciples are caught in a dreadful storm and their boat begins to fill with water. After being woken, Jesus rebukes the wind and the rain and the tempest passes. The disciples are perturbed, much to Jesus' dismay.

● **Casting Demons Into a Herd of Pigs**
A possessed man, able to burst free of his chains when restrained, is exorcised by Jesus. The demons ask to be sent into a herd of pigs but, while Jesus accommodates the request, the animals run down a hill and drown.

"Jesus feels able to forgive sins and his exorcisms demonstrate that evil can already be banished"

Quite when this transformation will occur is hard to tell. At times, Jesus locates it in the future ("thy kingdom come" as the famous line puts it), though it may happen quite soon: "the time is fulfilled and the kingdom of God is near." (Mark 1:15) Sometimes, though, Jesus gives a sense that the kingdom may already be in its early stages. He feels able to forgive sins and his exorcisms demonstrate that evil can already

be banished: "If it is by the finger of God that I drive out demons, then the kingdom of God has come upon you." (Matthew 12:28) To return to the parables: the mustard seed has been planted and the yeast is already in the bread mix.

Jesus is usually very cautious and enigmatic when it comes to identifying himself as the Messiah who will inaugurate the new age, but mere mention of a word like

"kingdom" was always likely to arouse the ire and suspicion of the Roman and Jewish authorities. This went a long way towards allowing those authorities to perceive Jesus as a threat: a would-be King of the Jews. On the two occasions when this term is applied to him, disaster ensues: first, at the outset when it leads to the Massacre of the Innocents, and then at the end, during the encounter with Pilate. On the other hand, nor does Jesus avoid provocative actions upon occasion. He cleanses the Temple, he enters Jerusalem in triumph, and he launches into criticism of the Pharisees. In the so-called Discourse on Defilement, Jesus denounces

● **Feeding the 5,000**
Jesus asks his disciples to feed the crowds who have followed him but no refreshments are available. Jesus takes five loaves and two fish and produces enough food for all. There are even some leftovers.

● **Walking on Water**
Jesus has spent the night in prayer. As the disciples return from the other side of the Sea of Galilee they see, much to their amazement, Jesus walking across the water. In one version, Peter attempts to emulate Jesus but, as his faith evaporates, he sinks.

● **The Blind Man of Bethsaida**
Jesus takes a blind man out of town, rubs spittle in his eye, and a miraculous cure ensues. Jesus has to make two attempts at this miracle, perhaps indicating that faith must be strived for.

● **Cleansing the Ten Lepers**
Leprosy was often seen as a punishment for sin and, in this miracle, Jesus cures ten afflicted men during his journey to Jerusalem. He is disappointed that nine of the men simply walk on and that only a Samaritan expresses gratitude.

● **Raising Lazarus**
News arrives that a friend of Jesus and the disciples is dying. By the time they reach him he has already been buried for four days. The stone is removed from the grave and Jesus orders Lazarus to arise, which he promptly does.

● **Withering the Fig Tree**
Jesus has recently arrived in Jerusalem. He goes to a fig tree in search of a snack but it carries no ripe fruit. He curses the tree, declaring that it will never bear fruit again. By the next morning the plant has withered away entirely.

The Transfiguration

Almost all the miracles described in the Gospels are about Jesus coming to the aid of other people. With The Transfiguration, however, Jesus becomes the main focus of the story. In the company of three of his disciples (James, John, and Peter), Jesus climbs to the top of a mountain (identified as Mount Tabor by later tradition). A dazzling, radiant light effects an extraordinary transformation with Jesus' "face shining as the sun" and his garments "as white as the light." (Matthew 17:2) Next, two of the Bible's most celebrated prophets, Moses and Elijah, appear beside Jesus. Peter suggests that tents should be erected, presumably to prolong this wondrous encounter, but then a voice speaks from a cloud declaring that this is his beloved son. Now, the disciples cannot see Moses or Elijah, so the heavenly voice is clearly referring to Jesus. The prophetic torch is not simply being passed from the old to the new, but Jesus' superiority is being announced. The reader is also encouraged to perceive a foreshadowing of the glory that will be granted to Jesus after his resurrection. ∎

Raphael's portrayal of The Transfiguration. The three disciples can be seen atop the mountain, rather overwhelmed by events

their prideful behavior—relishing the best seats at feasts, luxuriating in their fancy clothing—and itemizes the ways in which they are subverting the essence of Jewish law and teaching and forgetting that it is the inner man that truly counts. They are, he says, like "whitewashed tombs, beautiful on the outside but full of dead men's bones." (Matthew 23:27) Moreover, as the Gospels reveal, the Pharisees often "perceived that he had told [a] parable against them." (Mark 12:12)

This leads to an important final point. Christianity would, of course, grow into a worldwide religion, but Jesus' ministry must be understood in the Jewish context of 1st-century Palestine. Jesus encountered Gentiles, but his message was aimed squarely at his fellow Jews. His God was the God of the Hebrew Scriptures and he fully accepted the idea of the children of Israel being God's chosen people. He located his ideas within the parameters of Jewish law and, in part, it was his attempt to refine that tradition (and point out what he regarded as the abuses of the tradition) that so aggravated the Pharisees. Who was he, they asked, to dine with sinners and tax collectors or question the enforcement of ritual law?

For all that, aspects of Jesus' message as reported in the Gospels transcended the narrow limits of their time and place. Another kind of radicalism, one that sought to query the divisions of class and status, was also in evidence. "When you give a banquet, invite the poor, the crippled, the lame, and the blind." (Luke 14:13) This,

no doubt, was perceived as dangerous, too. Jesus was not bashful, because he naturally wanted to spread his ideas across the lands. We should not be surprised, therefore, that he provoked the anger of the powers-that-were. But this, from the perspective of those who came to worship him over the subsequent two millennia, was the inevitable end-point of his life's work.

The historian, of course, must seek to determine how far the Gospels reflect the reality of what truly happened during Jesus' life. This is an unenviable task. Some have suggested that, when it comes to the miracles and the parables, everything is sometimes a little too neat and tidy. Stories are conveniently grouped together to hammer home particular themes, and the language can become rather formulaic. At the very least, it is argued, a hefty measure of editorial intervention can be discerned. Contrariwise, the discrepancies between the Gospel accounts (parables and miracles in one text but not another; the conflation of episodes in some cases) can hardly be ignored, though this may only demonstrate that a particular Gospel writer wanted to highlight certain aspects of Jesus' message. On balance, we can probably conclude that many aspects of Jesus' ministry as depicted in the Gospels bear a tolerable resemblance to what actually transpired. He most likely told those kinds of stories and claimed to have performed those kinds of miracles—whether you choose to believe in them or not!

A panel by Jan Polack shows Christ in full flow, preaching in the temple

Icon of the Raising of Lazarus

Artist: Byzantine School
Year: Pre-1453

The Renaissance might be the most famous period of religious art, but Byzantine art was almost exclusively concerned with depicting scenes from the history of Christianity. In this icon of the Raising of Lazarus (likely created before the fall of Constantinople), Lazarus is swaddled in bandages in his opened sarcophagus, with Jesus facing him. Icons of Christ, the saints, or the Virgin Mary were essential in churches, and most homes would feature them.

The Cleansing of the Temple

Jesus was angered to see the way the Temple of Jerusalem was being used and cast out the businessmen occupying the forecourt to make space to preach to all nations

WRITTEN BY CHARLIE EVANS

The Cleansing of the Temple is the infamous event in the Bible where Jesus drives out the merchants and money changers from the Temple. Unlike many biblical narratives, all of the Gospels of the New Testament describe Jesus and his disciples arriving in Jerusalem for Passover. The holiday occuring in spring commemorates the liberation of the Jews as slaves in Ancient Egypt. The canonical Gospels explain how Jesus arrived at a courtyard in the Temple in Jerusalem, a series of buildings situated on the Temple Mount in the Old City of Jerusalem, and was angered by the activities at the sacred site. He found the area was busy with livestock, merchants, and money changers whose business was to exchange Greek and Roman currency for Jewish and Tyrian money. The holy location, which was built to worship God, was being taken advantage of by greedy businessmen who saw the opportunity to make money. Rather than a house of God, it had become a market. Angered that the people were making a mockery of his Father's house, Jesus made a short whip to move out the animals and shopkeepers and "drove out all who sold and bought in the temple." (Matthew 21:12) People were outraged as he pushed over all the tables and said, "It is written, 'My house shall be called a house of prayer,' but you make it a den of robbers." (Matthew 21:13)

The Significance of the Cleansing of the Temple

Jesus' disruption at the Temple has been widely discussed by scholars. What was once interpreted as rebellion against the religious authorities has since been disputed. Instead, it is thought that Jesus was angered to see exploitative businessmen taking advantage of the poor and disrespecting the purpose-built place of worship. Mark highlights that Jesus did not intend to completely purge the Temple of all business transactions, but that he wanted to restore the atmosphere solemnity in the areas that were reserved for all the nations (non-Jews and Jews alike) as he said: "My house shall be called a house of prayer for all the nations." This is because the business activity was happening in the outer circle of the Temple, the area reserved for everyone, and Jesus was angered that it had encroached on the area where non-Jews were allowed to come and pray. He wanted to fulfil Isaiah's vision of universalism. This is why he uses the phrase "den of robbers"—it was a cleverly crafted almost-threat describing the exploitative businessmen. He was referring to Jeremiah (7), which chronicles a doomed corrupt priesthood that was destroyed. It was an eerie foreshadowing that soon Jesus would tear down the old ways of worship and replace it with his message. It is thought that the authorities were unable to fight back when Jesus cleared the Temple, as the everyday people loved him as Messiah. The authorities had no wish to create a civil war and wanted to keep the peace, but scholars expect that his rebellion started sowing the seeds of their plots to get rid of Jesus.

Jesus' Message

After the Temple was cleared of the people using it as a passageway and for commercial trade, Jesus wanted to teach his message. Scholars expect that he would have done so from the Royal Stoa—a covered porch on the southern part of the Temple Mount. This part of the outer circle was open to non-Jews and allowed him to preach his word. Jesus has spent his short years as a preacher talking about the word of God and forgiving people for their sins, a new way that meant people didn't have to slaughter an animal in the name of God. Although he recognized that the Temple was a true signpost to God's will, he saw it right for destruction because his way of doing things was new and different, and more in allegiance with the Holy Spirit. He was replacing the traditional way of repentance as a symbolic protest that seriously challenged the norms of the time, and made it clear to the authorities that held reign that they were under judgement.

Jesus wasn't following the trend throughout his entire time teaching his message and was going against the grains of society. When he arrived at the Temple, he disagreed with who was representing the coming kingdom of God. His dismantling of the Temple was a critique of the higher authorities and the oppressive structure under which the building was run, where the high priests were living at a detriment to the poorer worshippers who were left to be exploited by businessmen. The event was a turning point in his story; it is likely that Jesus' rebellious actions that day sealed his fate on the cross; "And the chief priests and the scribes heard it and were seeking a way to destroy him, for they feared him, because all the crowd was astonished at his teaching." (Mark 11:18)

The Temple in Jerusalem

The Temple in Jerusalem was a series of ornate structures built on the Temple Mount in the Old City of Jerusalem. Today, Dome of the Rock and Al-Aqsa Mosque are located on the site. According to the Old Testament, the First Temple was built long before Jesus' time, in 957 BCE. It was constructed by King Solomon but destroyed several years later by Shoshenq, Pharaoh of Egypt. The building that Jesus cleansed had been built in 538 BCE and had been commissioned by Cyrus the Great after the fall of the Babylonian Empire. It was later renovated by Herod the Great in 20 BCE, and was ultimately destroyed during the Siege of Jerusalem by the Romans in 70 CE. Following the Muslim conquest of Jerusalem during the 7th Century, an Islamic shrine and a mosque was built on the site. In more recent history, the Temple Mount was captured by Israel from Jordan in 1967 and Jews were able to return to pray at the holy site. ■

The site as it sits today after a history of conquests and rebuilding

Jesus consecrates the sacred host in Juan de Juanes' *La Sagrada Cena*

The Final Showdown

Jesus prepares his followers for his arrest and also for their life afterwards

WRITTEN BY DEREK WILSON

A term often used by theologians in relation to the biblical narrative is *Sitz im Leben*, a German expression which translates literally as "setting in life" or "historical context." If we are to get most out of a text, we need to know not only what it is saying but who it is saying it to. For whom was it originally written and what were their circumstances? In no instance is that more important than when we are thinking about the Last Supper, the meal Jesus shared with his closest followers on the eve of his trial and summary execution. The emotionally charged narrative is of enormous significance as a kind of spiritual 'bridge' between the earthly ministry of Jesus and the life of the early Church. But at the same time, it vitally connects the life of the emerging Christian Church with the life of the people of God in the Old Testament. Every element of the story, therefore, has to be understood in terms of its place in history.

The first back reference to note is that the meal took place at Passovertide. Passover was the most important ritual event in the Jewish year, and was intended to be a perpetual reminder of the Israelites' deliverance from slavery in Egypt. On the night preceding their mass departure under Moses' leadership, every household was to kill a sheep or goat and eat it. The animal's blood was to be smeared on the doorposts and lintel of every house to identify those who were God's people (Exodus 12). Jewish families annually reenacted the eating of the Passover meal and, by so doing, declared their religious identity. The Passover celebration lasted for a week, and there is

some disagreement among scholars about exactly when the Last Supper occurred. Some suggest that the Last Supper was a fellowship meal that took place during the festival. Most, however, agree that it was the Passover meal at which the sacrificial lamb was eaten. What is not disputed is that Jesus deliberately gave a new meaning to the idea of God's deliverance of his chosen people.

Within the New Testament, there are five descriptions of the Last Supper. The first was written by St. Paul in 1 Corinthians in the mid-50s CE, by which time Christianity had spread with remarkable rapidity throughout the Mediterranean world. In the cosmopolitan Greek port of Corinth, most Christians were Gentiles, and the essential 'Jewishness' of what had come to be called the 'Lord's Supper' had somewhat faded. It seems to have become a celebration feast in which some participants gorged themselves or got drunk. Paul reminded them of the significance of the central feature of the meal: "On the night he was betrayed, the Lord Jesus took a piece of bread, gave thanks to God, broke it, and said, 'This is my body which is for you. Do this in memory of me.' In the same way, after the supper he took the cup and said, 'This cup is God's new covenant, sealed with my blood. Whenever you drink it, do so in memory of me.' (1 Corinthians 11:23-25)

Not very long after this (c. 55-75 CE), the 'synoptic' Gospels of Matthew, Mark, and Luke were in circulation in the churches. They were written to provide believers with a fuller account of the life and ministry of Jesus. When it came to the Last Supper, all the writers, like Paul, highlighted the concept of the covenant. This was a fundamental, exclusive arrangement between God and his chosen people, an agreement based on mutual obligations. During the years after the escape from Egypt, when the Israelites were living as nomads in the Sinai Peninsula, God, through Moses, pledged his protection and support in return for the loyalty of the people, signified by their keeping of moral laws and ritual practices, based on the Ten Commandments. As in the Passover, animal sacrifice and the sprinkling of blood featured in the ceremony sealing the covenant. Then, some 650 years later, the prophet Jeremiah announced God's intention to negotiate a new covenant. Unlike the elaborate written law code Moses gave the people, the terms of this agreement would be "written on their hearts." God's chosen would instinctively know right from wrong. Even if they failed, God assured them of his "forgiveness." (Jeremiah 31:31) At the Last Supper, Jesus told his disciples that he was inaugurating this new covenant. Like the old one, it would be sealed with a sacrifice—his own. His blood would be shed. And his people would drink it, not in actuality but symbolically, by sharing the cup of wine. "Drink it, all of you," he instructed. "This is my blood which seals God's covenant, my blood poured out for many for the forgiveness of sins." (Matthew 26:27-8)

The Chosen Ones

In John's Gospel, the last to be written (c 90-100 CE), five whole chapters were devoted to the Last Supper. It included no account of the sharing of bread and wine, which by now was celebrated in all the Christian churches. The writer saw no need to tell his fellow believers what they already knew. However, there was a lot he had to say that many of them did not know. The fourth Gospel account was all about the Church, the fellowship of believers, its founding fathers, their frailty, and the transformation that came over them at that first Easter. These were the new 'chosen people' and the writer made the point straight away: "Jesus knew that the hour had come for him to leave this world and go to the Father. He had always loved those in the world who were his own, and he loved them to the very end." (John 13:1) The Passover meal, presumably, followed its traditional pattern until Jesus did something quite unexpected. He girded himself with a towel, took a bowl of water and washed the disciples' feet. Jesus' action (usually that of a servant) disturbed the 12 recipients. Peter voiced their protest. By way of explanation Jesus said, "I have set you an example; this is the kind of humble service you should all perform for one another."

"The disciples were still thinking in terms of an earthly king who would hand out positions of power"

The messiah the Jews were expecting was a political figure, and the disciples were still thinking in terms of an earthly king who would hand out positions of power to his lieutenants. Only recently they had been arguing about their relative positions in the new order. Jesus' vision of his future 'kingdom' was of one whose citizens would be marked out by mutual love and service.

What came next was even more disturbing. "One of you," Jesus said, "is going to betray me." It was not just the unity and harmony of the little group that was in question; one of them was actually a traitor. We can imagine the questions, suspicions, and recriminations running around the table. The Renaissance artist, Leonardo da Vinci in his famous painting, The Last Supper, captured this very moment. He showed the shocked faces and the gesticulations of the 12 men as they responded to this terrible accusation. They pressed Jesus to identify the turncoat. He gave a sign to indicate Judas Iscariot and told him to "be quick about it." Somehow, the others failed to grasp the significance of this.

The motivation of Judas has been debated for centuries. Was he overcome by simple greed? He was the group's money man and looked after the common purse. It seems that he did not always agree with Jesus about how the funds should be spent. Some scholars suggest that the disillusionment went further; that Judas was a rabid nationalist who had grasped, ahead of the others, that Jesus was not going to be the political savior who would deliver the Jews from Roman oppression. If anyone was a traitor, he may have argued, it was Jesus. He had deceived his followers into believing that they were part of an uprising that he had no intention of launching. So, Judas decided to change sides and pocket a tidy sum in the process.

Then again, there have been some thinkers who have turned this line of reasoning on its head. Their interpretation runs like this: at the supper, Jesus made

Thomas is seated to Christ's left in Da Vinci's *The Last Supper*

clear that he knew what Judas was contemplating and he actually told him to get on and do it. Perhaps, then, Judas thought, arrest was part of the plan. It would be the signal for rebellion. The atmosphere in the city was tense. Days before, Jesus had been welcomed by a jubilant crowd. If the people's hero was arrested, that would set off the explosion. It was all part of Jesus' plan.

That version may be too subtle, but it does, in some respects, come closest to what most Christians believe about Jesus' betrayal. The Messiah knew that he would be put to death. It was something foretold by the prophets. The synoptic Gospels (Matthew, Mark, and Luke) all record words of Jesus that bluntly set side-by-side the inevitability of the betrayal: "The Son of Man must be betrayed but how terrible it will be for the one who betrays him." (Matthew 26:24)

After Judas's departure, Jesus tried to prepare the remaining 11 for their coming ordeal. What followed in the narrative of the Last Supper were messages both of challenge and reassurance. Jesus spoke of "comings and going." He will go away—into death—but he will return from death.

This would enable his followers to make that same journey and rob 'death' of its terrors because Jesus would provide 'abodes' or 'resting places' for believers in the world beyond (John 14:1-4). But Jesus spoke here, for the first time, of another kind of 'going' and 'coming'. Eventually, his physical presence in this world would cease but he would return to his followers and indwell them by his spirit.

This revolutionary new teaching (John 14:15-25; 16: 4-15) is fundamental to any understanding of how the early Christian Church survived. At the Last Supper, Jesus pulled no punches: "If you belonged to the world, then the world would love you as its own. But I chose you from this world . . . that is why the world hates you." (John 15:19) Those words would certainly have struck a chord with the first readers, who in the light of bitter experience, recognized fulfilled prophecy in them. But with Jesus' warning, there also came reassurance: he would send them a 'helper' (John 16:7-15). The word used in the original Greek was *paraclete*, variously translated as "helper," "counselor," or "advocate." The connotation

Breaking the Bread Becomes High Drama

Luke's Gospel (24:28-32) contains an extraordinary postscript to the Last Supper and one which caught the imagination of the Renaissance artist Michelangelo Merisi da Caravaggio (1571-1610). Three days after the crucifixion, two disciples were walking the seven miles from Jerusalem to the village of Emmaus when they were joined by a fellow traveler they did not recognize. They were probably members of the wider group of Jesus' followers who did not know him as intimately as the Twelve. The 'stranger' was also the last person they ever expected to see. As they walked, he explained the Old Testament references to the suffering messiah. At Emmaus, the three sat down for a meal. It was as Jesus blessed the bread and broke it that the 'penny dropped'. Was there something distinctive about the way he performed these simple acts? Whatever the reason, the moment of recognition was highly dramatic and Caravaggio captured the mood of the moment in his famous painting. One disciple flings his arms wide in astonishment. The other is about to leap from his chair. Even the bowl of fruit seems about to fall off the table. ■

"He had deceived his followers into believing they were part of an uprising he had no intention of launching"

is a legal one, indicating an aid who gives support and advice to defendants in court. This tied in with the prophecy of Jeremiah.

Into the Night

The crisis was now at hand. Jesus' last act at the supper was to pray for his followers. Again, we are reminded of the Sitz im Leben, for, having asked a blessing on the 11 loyal disciples, Jesus added: "I pray not only for them, but also for those who believe in me because of their message. I pray that they may all be one." (John 17:20-1) The writer was passing on Jesus' message that unity was vital. By now, night had fallen and Jesus led his followers to one of their favorite haunts. They went across the Kidron Valley, to the east of the Temple Mount and crossed to a grove known as the Mount of Olives. There, Jesus left his companions resting, taking only Peter, James, and John to keep watch while he prayed to prepare himself for the ordeal to come. The three heard him crying out for the burden to be lifted but submitting to God's will. According to Luke's Gospel, they saw the sweat dripping from his brow like drops of blood. Overwhelmed themselves, they fell into an exhausted sleep.

Too late, they saw Judas arrive leading a torchlit posse of Jewish temple guards and Roman soldiers to arrest Jesus. The traitor identified Jesus to the soldiers with a 'Judas kiss'. There was a scuffle in which the disciples made a futile attempt to rescue their leader before running off into the night.

Jesus was taken straight to the house of Annas, the leader of the high-priestly family and the leading political figure in Jerusalem. The actual high priest in that year was his son-in-law, Caiaphas, but it was Annas who pulled the strings and the Jewish council, the Sanhedrin, would, in all likelihood, follow his lead. Annas had many political factors to weigh up—the mood of the Jerusalem populace, the strength of Jesus' following, and the attitude of the Roman governor. He would want to be sure of his ground before proceeding further. His concerns were purely political. The old man asked who Jesus' followers were and what he was teaching them. Jesus replied that there was nothing covert about his actions and that the authorities could have challenged him openly at any time (in fact, they had often done so). Annas concluded after a brief examination that there was no band of armed men waiting in the hills to come to their leader's rescue, and that the prisoner could safely be sent for interrogation by the full Sanhedrin.

The accounts of this interrogation vary slightly in the Gospel narratives, but

"The accusers went to great lengths to find witnesses prepared to perjure themselves"

Annas Confronts Jesus–but Who is Really in Control?

Gerrit van Honthorst's painting of *Christ Before the High Priest*, right, (c.1617) might almost be subtitled *A Study in Silence*. The artist captures the night-time scene of Jesus' interrogation by Annas. The religious politician fired questions, hoping to intimidate his prisoner but, as far as we know, Jesus' only reply was "My ministry has been public, you could have challenged me any time." The impression van Honthorst conveys is that it is not Annas who is in command of the situation. Jesus is, by this time, quite ready for the ordeal to come. He embraces it. Against his wall of silent composure, Annas's loaded questions can only bounce back. ∎

what is clear is that the objective of the council was to find an excuse to get Jesus condemned and delivered to the secular power (the Roman governor) as quickly as possible to avoid any popular backlash. The accusers went to great lengths to find witnesses prepared to perjure themselves by giving false testimony. They produced two witnesses who claimed that Jesus had thrown out a challenge: "Pull the Temple down and I will miraculously build it in three days." This was a distortion of a statement Jesus had actually made about a different kind of 'temple'—his own body. He refused to answer the allegation. Eventually, Caiaphas challenged him directly with the big question: "Are you the Messiah, the Son of the Blessed God?" Jesus had not openly claimed this title, but it was what others were saying about him, including many who had welcomed him rapturously into the city a few days before, but he would not avoid the direct question. He said, "I am, and you will see the Son of Man seated on the right of the Almighty and coming with the clouds of heaven." "Blasphemy!" The councillors shouted. "He deserves the death penalty!" (Mark 15:61-2)

The politico-religious background to Jesus' condemnation may need some clarifying. The Jews were expecting the Messiah, a king who would deliver them from foreign oppression. Several such figures had appeared from time to time making false claims. The Jewish leaders were walking on eggshells—while not wanting to abandon the hope of a divine deliverer, they were terrified of upsetting the Romans and making the political situation worse. Jesus' acknowledgement of his messiahship was not a claim to temporal power. The new covenant he proclaimed was to establish the Kingdom of God in people's hearts. The politicians were never going to grasp the subtlety of Jesus' brand of messiahship. Therefore, it could only be established by his death.

The Last Supper
Artist: Leonardo da Vinci
Year: 1495-98

According to the Gospel of John, Jesus is painted with his disciples for their last supper. Here, da Vinci depicts the moment that Jesus reveals that one among them will betray him. Shocked, his disciples exhibit a range of reactions, from anger, surprise, disbelief, and seeking reassurance. Judas, fourth from the left with his elbow on table, leans back and stares at Jesus, perhaps aghast at the revelation of the plan. For centuries the Last Supper had been a popular religious scene in art, but da Vinci's scene was an innovative take on the story, with the artist focusing on the raw emotion triggered by such an evocative statement.

Pontius Pilate

Roman governors are not usually remembered in history. This one was

WRITTEN BY EDOARDO ALBERT

Herod the Great ruled Judea effectively for his Roman overseers for around 35 years. This was the preferred Roman method for governing difficult parts of their empire: find a local strongman beholden to them, who could be supported so long as he kept everything quiet and cut loose if things went wrong. From the Roman point of view, everything went right under Herod: he dealt with his people in their vernacular, linguistically and culturally, while keeping the taxes flowing to Rome. Indeed, so satisfied were they with the arrangements that after Herod's death Augustus allowed the provisions of Herod's will to stand, with the kingdom being parceled out among three of his four surviving sons (being a child of Herod was risky business: he had executed his three eldest sons). However, Augustus came to regret part of Herod's disposition fairly quickly when one son, Herod Archelaus, who had received the part of the kingdom including Jerusalem, proved so incompetent and violent a ruler that Augustus had to remove him and impose direct Roman rule.

What Did the Romans Ever Do for Us?

Under Augustus, Judea was ruled by governors, known as prefects, who were moved to a different post after three years to try to keep corruption low level and to prevent the prefects building up local power bases. But Augustus' successor as emperor, Tiberius, changed the policy and allowed prefects to stay on station longer for the cynical reason, as he remarked, that once a fly had sucked its fill from a wound, it was better to let it stay there and keep the other flies away. For patrician Romans, an appointment to a prefecture was often seen as a sinecure, an easy way to lay up riches. However, the prefects of Judea

quickly learned that that was not the case with their volatile province. Pilate was the fifth Roman prefect; he was deposed as governor of Judea in 36/37 CE, although there is some doubt as to when he became prefect in the first place. Working from Josephus, the Jewish historian, most scholars dated the start of his rule to 26 CE, but this has recently been revised earlier by some historians, giving a start to Pilate's governorship in 18/19 CE. This would also align well with the long spell as Temple high priest served by Caiaphas, who was removed from his role at the same time that Pilate was deposed. Previously, high priests had served for as short a period as the governing prefect. Reading behind the sources, we can surmise that Pilate eased Caiaphas' path to the top job on the understanding that Caiaphas would cooperate with the governor: then when Pilate fell, Caiaphas went down too.

As governor of Judea, our sources—the historian Josephus and the philosopher Philo—paint a consistent picture of Pilate as an autocratic ruler subject to sudden changes of mind when he realized that he had overreached himself. This is best exemplified in Pilate's attempt to impose Roman practices upon the Jews. The previous prefects had been scrupulous in avoiding offending Jewish religious sensibilities; in particular, they had their soldiers cover the legion standards when they entered Jerusalem. The statues of eagles or busts of the emperor broke the Jewish prohibition against images. But Pilate had his troops enter Jerusalem with their standards uncovered. However, in a premeditated

Defining Moment

Trial of a Jewish Prophet
The Sanhedrin did not have the authority to condemn a man to death. So, Jesus was brought before Pilate and though, according to the Gospels, he could find no guilt, Pilate decided it was better an innocent man die than his governorship be troubled. Having had Jesus flogged, he handed him over for execution by crucifixion: the punishment inflicted by the Romans on slaves and rebels.
30-33 CE

Ecce Homo by Antonio Ciseri depicts Pilate addressing the crowd before the crucifixion is ordered

move, he had them do this at night, so that the populace would not see them marching in with their standards held high. By the time the people of Jerusalem realized what was happening, the soldiers were secure in the Antonia Fortress, the stronghold that dominated the city, from where they flaunted their standards.

Although Pilate had ordered this, he took care to ensure he was personally out of harm's way, being in residence in Caesarea when his men went into Jerusalem. However, when the Jews saw the Roman troops flouting their religious law, many went to Pilate in Caesarea to plead with him to remove the offending imperial standards. For five days, delegations met Pilate and for five days he refused, arguing that it would be an outrage to the emperor to remove the standards once they had been put in place. Growing tired of their supplications, on the sixth day Pilate had his troops hidden around the stadium where he gave his audiences. When the Jewish leaders again presented themselves to argue their case, Pilate gave the signal and his soldiers surrounded the Jews. Turning to the supplicants in front of him, Pilate said that they would be put to death if they did not put aside their complaints and accept the imperial standards as a fait accompli. At this, the Jewish delegation bared their throats to the soldiers' swords and said they would rather die than accept the abrogation of their ancient laws by Pilate. When Pilate saw this and realized the chaos that would ensue if he executed so much of the higher echelons of Jewish society, he backed off, and brought the imperial standards back to Caesarea.

Such was often the pattern of Pilate's governorship: he would push against

This Roman bust is said to portray Josephus, the Jewish historian from whom we learn most about Pilate's wider career as prefect of Judea

Jewish sensibilities—whether through ignorance or in an attempt to establish his authority is unclear— and then, when the Jews pushed back, he would back off. These are the marks of a man unsure of his power and his position— and himself.

However, on a later occasion, when Pilate pushed Jewish religious sensibilities, he did so with a murderously violent response already planned. The occasion was Pilate's use of a Jewish religious tax to fund construction of an aqueduct. Expecting a Jewish response, Pilate had arranged for soldiers in civilian clothes to mingle with the crowd, armed with clubs and cudgels. From his seat on the tribunal, Pilate gave the signal, and the soldiers started laying about them with their clubs. According to Josephus, many Jews died either from being beaten or in the stampede to get away.

The Grand Alliance

None of our sources suggest that the Temple authorities had any difficulties with Pilate's appropriation of the Temple tax to pay for the aqueduct—indeed, the

Some of the earliest depictions of Pilate are in mosaics. This dates from the 5th or 6th century and is in Sant'Apollinare Nuovo in Ravenna

According to Matthew's Gospel, Pilate washed his hands in an attempt to excuse himself from the guilt of condemning an innocent man to death

The Pilate Stone

Apart from the documentary sources, there is archaeological proof of Pilate's historicity in the roughly square shape of a limestone block, excavated in 1961 from the Herodian theater in Ancient Caesarea. The block had been part of a staircase but, turning it over, the archaeologists found an inscription on it which read (conjectural letters in brackets):

[Dis Augusti]s Tiberiéum
[—Po]ntius Pilatus
[praef]ectus Iuda[ea]e
[fecit, d]é[dicavit]

This can be translated as: "[Po]ntius Pilate, [pref] ect of Jud[e]a, [made and d]e[dicated] Tiberieum to the [divine August]us." The Tiberieum, presumably erected in honor of Emperor Tiberius, had been demolished and the dedication stone re-used four centuries later. Apart from confirming Pilate's existence as governor, the Pilate stone has also served to correct our documentary sources. The Roman historian Tacitus, writing c. 116, said, "Christus, from whom the name had its origin, suffered the extreme penalty during the reign of Tiberius at the hands of one of our procurators, Pontius Pilatus." Following Tacitus, later writers assumed that Pilate was procurator of Judea, but in the early 1st century, procurators had financial responsibilities while prefects were military governors. Thus, we now know that Pilate was prefect of Judea, not its procurator. ■

The Pilate stone measures 32 by 27 inches and it is kept at the Israel Museum in Jerusalem

Sadducean priests saw the half-shekel tax as a Pharisaic innovation. So here we see further evidence for a commonality of interest between Pilate and Caiaphas. Something close to confirmation of this is provided by what happened after Pilate's eventual downfall.

Sporadic outbursts of violence had characterized Pilate's prefecture, and it was another that brought about his removal. This time, it was the Samaritans (now known through being proverbial, but originally Israelites who had intermarried with non-Jews and had settled in the northern part of the kingdom) who suffered from Pilate's violent overreaction. Suspecting a revolt, Pilate sent his troops to Mount Gerizim, which the Samaritans believed God had ordained for his worship rather than the Temple Mount in Jerusalem, and executed the Samaritan leaders while treating the ordinary Samaritans with exemplary brutality. The Samaritans who survived complained to Pilate's superior, the Roman legate of Syria, who removed Pilate from his position and ordered him to face charges in front of Emperor Tiberius. However, for Pilate's good fortune, Tiberius died while he was on his way to Rome.

Having removed Pilate, the Syrian legate, Vitellius, went to Jerusalem and removed

Caiaphas. The proximity of the two sackings strongly suggest that there was an informal alliance between the two men, one that Vitellius decided to end.

As to the final fate of Pontius Pilate, little is known for certain. Much later, various Christian traditions suggested that he committed suicide when ordered to do so by Caligula, or that he died, again by suicide, while in exile, but all of these traditions are far removed from the time of Pilate's death and rendered suspect by Christian apologists engaging in polemics with pagan philosophers and needing to concoct a suitably grisly death for the deicide. No contemporary or near-contemporary source says anything further about the fate of the prefect who, though convinced of the innocence of the man brought before him, decided to put expedience before justice and have him executed. There were likely many other such prefects during the Empire, but Pontius Pilate, by virtue of this decision, is the only one remembered through the centuries.

Thus, the picture of Pilate that emerges from secular sources chimes closely with his portrayal in the Gospels: a man who vacillated when faced with determined opposition, and a ruler more than prepared to overcompensate for his inadequacies by employing extreme violence

Defining Moment

Water, Water

Archaeologists believe they have identified the aqueduct for which Pilate appropriated Temple funds as a branch of the system of aqueducts bringing water to Jerusalem. The aqueduct runs from the Arrub spring south of Bethlehem and feeds Solomon's Pools. The aqueduct runs for 24 miles, taking many meanders so that it does not require tunnels, bridges, or pipes.

1st century CE

to meet his ends. Pilate had little regard for the sensibilities or the lives of the people he governed. As prefect of Judea, he was committed to maintaining Roman rule and was quite prepared to sacrifice the innocent in order to do so. However, it was this combination of ruthlessness and lack of control that eventually brought about his downfall, when Pilate acted murderously on the basis of false rumors about a Samaritan revolt.

It was one of Jesus' many accomplishments that he managed to unite against him so many people and groups who normally hated each other: while Pilate and the Sadduccean priesthood were allies, they were loathed by the Pharisees and the Herodians. But they all joined together to rid themselves of this troublesome prophet who threatened to upset all their apple carts.

Herod Antipas

The son of Herod the Great clung to power with as much tenacity as his father, but would have been forgotten save for a drunken promise and an unexpected encounter with a condemned man

WRITTEN BY ROBIN GRIFFITH-JONES

The Jews presented a paradox to the Roman authorities. Stubbornly monotheistic in a world where gods multiplied more quickly than Xs in Roman numerals, they were the prickliest of subjects and the most trusted of citizens. For the Jews of the Empire fell into two quite distinct groups: the Diaspora Jews, living outside Palestine, who were rich, cosmopolitan, literate, and interested in ideas, above all the dialogue with Hellenic thought. And then there were the Jews of Palestine. These were seen by the authorities as disputatious and dangerous, a stiff-necked and obdurate people who could take violent umbrage at some unsuspected flouting of one of their innumerable laws. But a token of how highly the Diaspora Jews were regarded by the Roman authorities is the fact that Jews were granted dispensation from the state-sanctioned, indeed the state-required, worship of the emperor. Rather than offering sacrifice to the emperor, the Jews were allowed to offer sacrifices for him and his well-being. No other people were granted such a concession.

To square this Jewish circle, the preferred Roman response was to recruit an insider. In Herod the Great, they found the ideal placeman. Herod took the throne of Judea in 43 BCE, and the Romans recognized him as king four years later. While Herod was, to those closest to him, a monster, he was generous to his people, both those in Judea and the Diaspora. In Jerusalem, he rebuilt the Temple in magnificence, drawing wonder-struck tourists from throughout the Empire, while in the Empire, he personally endowed Jewish community centers and synagogues. Indeed, so successful was

his rule that Augustus acquiesced to the division, in his will, of his kingdom between his three surviving sons: Herod Archelaus, Herod Philip and Herod Antipas. Archelaus got Judea but proved such a disastrous administrator of Jerusalem and its hinterland that the Romans deposed him and imposed direct rule through prefects, of whom the fifth was Pilate.

Herod Antipas, Herod the Great's youngest son, proved to be a far wilier operator than his elder brother, remaining ruler of Galilee and Perea for over 40 years. As ruler, he founded the city of Tiberias on the shore of the Sea of Galilee as his capital. Archaeological excavations around his realm indicate that he was sensitive to the religious sensibilities of his people, as there is no evidence that Roman temples, hippodromes, or gymnasia were built in his kingdom during his rule, although this changed dramatically following the Jewish Revolt from 66 to 70 CE and the destruction of the Temple. Outside the accounts in the Bible, Herod Antipas is attested historically in the histories of the great Jewish historian, Josephus, and archaeologists have found five coin series issued in his name, carrying the legend, "Of Herod the Tetrarch" in Greek. Mindful of the biblical prohibition against images, the coin series issued by Herod Antipas do not have his portrait but rather floral motifs. He is also named in a market weight excavated from Tiberias, which reads in Greek,

Defining Moment

The Death of Princes

Around 7 BCE, Herod put on trial his two sons, Alexander and Aristobulus, for treason before a court composed of his hirelings. Not surprisingly, the court found as Herod wished, and Herod put his two sons to death. Three years later, Herod's eldest son by his first wife, Antipater, was also executed for treason. The way was now open for Herod Antipas, son of Herod's third wife, to become ruler.

c. 7 BCE

Defining Moment

Roman Childhood
Herod Antipas spent most of his childhood in Rome. It was standard Roman policy to invite the children of client kings to Rome so that they might enjoy a Classical education and make contact with the upper echelons of society. It additionally served to remind the kings that failure to serve Rome properly would likely have fatal repercussions for their planned heirs.
c. 15 BCE

Dead Sea Fortress

The fortress of Machaerus, where Herod Antipas imprisoned John the Baptist, was built on a hill on the eastern shore of the Dead Sea by the second Hasmonean king, Alexander Jannaeus, around 90 BCE, then rebuilt by that inveterate builder, Herod the Great, in 30 BCE. With its commanding position, and the natural defense of surrounding ravines, the fortress made for both an excellent stronghold against attack from the east, and a vital communication node should an attack come, since signals from Machaerus were easily visible to the other fortresses on the west side of Judea. Archaeologists have discoverd a typically luxurious Herodian fortress/palace, with mosaics and carved limestone decorations. The fortress had bastions on three sides with walls that were 30 feet high, a cistern sunk 50 feet into the rock to store water, a Roman-style bath, and a triclinium, where guests would have reclined on couches for formal dining. The most striking feature is the peristyle courtyard, where the columns of an elegant porch marked out the cool enclosure. It was here, with his guests eased by the evening breeze, that Herod Antipas watched his stepdaughter dance. It seems that the breeze was not able to cool him enough. ■

The site of the hilltop palace fortress of Machaerus, with the Dead Sea in the background

"In the 34th year of Herod the Tetrarch, during the term of office as market overseer of Gaius Julius . . ." Taken together, these conclusively prove the historicity of Herod Antipas and his reign.

A Problem with Prophets

For more detail on the life of Herod Antipas, we have to look to the Gospel accounts. In these, he figures as a political operator, a manipulative schemer who is himself manipulated, most famously when his step-daughter, Salome, dances for him at his birthday party (Salome is not named in the accounts in Mark, Matthew, and Luke, but Josephus names her as stepdaughter to Herod Antipas in his Antiquities) (Mark 6:14-29, Matthew 14:1-12, Luke 9:7-9). John the Baptist had criticized the marriage between Herod Antipas and Herodias, the mother of Salome, on the grounds that it was unlawful, since Herodias was the niece of Herod Antipas, as well as having been previously married to his half-brother. John,

Defining Moment

The Father-in-Law

The first wife of Herod Antipas was Phasaelis, the daughter of Aretas, king of the Nabataeans. When Phasaelis learned that Herod Antipas intended to divorce her to marry Herodias, she fled to her father. Aretas, the enraged father-in-law, invaded and defeated the army of Herod Antipas. According to Josephus, many Jews blamed Herod's defeat on his execution of John the Baptist. **c. 30 CE**

a fierce figure preaching repentance, would have already aroused the attention of a ruler nervous of anyone arousing the passions of his volatile subjects—passions his Roman overseers expected Herod to keep damped down. But Antipas seems to have regarded John with a mixture of fascination and fear, imprisoning him at his fortress at Machaerus but remaining unsure of what to do about the threat he posed. The fortress is currently under excavation and archaeologists have discovered the very spot where Herod Antipas sat when Salome danced for him. In the axial center of a formal peristyle courtyard lined with porticoes is a semi-circular apse that would have held the king's throne.

Herodias, however, knew exactly what she wanted for this agitator against her marriage and her status. When Salome came to tell her that an evidently drunk Herod had promised her whatever she would have, up to half his kingdom, and had done so in front of witnesses, Herodias told her all-too dutiful daughter exactly what she

Al Pacino stars as Herod Antipas in an adaptation of Oscar Wilde's play *Salome*

Although not named in the Gospel accounts, Salome is attested in Josephus, and coins commemorating her and her second husband, Aristobulus, have been found

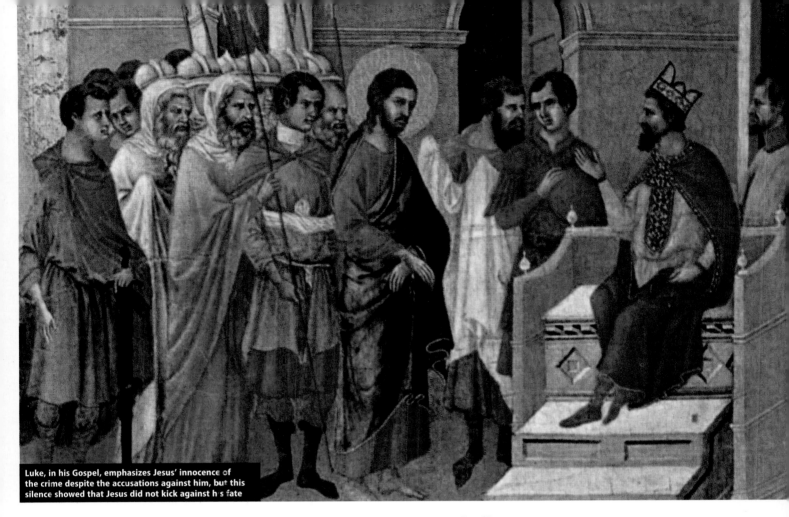

Luke, in his Gospel, emphasizes Jesus' innocence of the crime despite the accusations against him, but this silence showed that Jesus did not kick against his fate

"Pilate evidently had no wish to inflame an already volatile situation by putting a reputed Jewish prophet to death"

should ask for: the head of John the Baptist. Caught out by his public promise, Herod Antipas had little choice but to give Salome what she had asked for. On a plate.

The Fox

When a new prophet arose, Herod Antipas was caught unawares. There had been no prophets among the Jews for generations, and now here there was a second. Herod, possibly still guilty at executing John, thought that Jesus was John resurrected (Matthew 14:1-2, Mark 6:14-16). However, some of Herod's supporters decided it was best to deal with this new prophet in the traditional way: by killing him (Mark 3:6). According to Luke, Herod too plotted to kill Jesus. When news of this was brought to Jesus by some Pharisees, it prompted one of his most scathing replies: "Go tell that fox, 'I will drive out demons and heal people today and tomorrow, and on the third day I will reach my goal.'" The Aramaic word translated into Greek as 'fox' has a wider meaning in Jesus' tongue than just a crafty, wily animal. It also meant—to put it in modern terms—a pompous, ineffectual jerk. To the people listening, Jesus was saying that Herod Antipas had neither the

ability nor the power to put him to death. Nonetheless, when Jesus heard that Herod had executed John he withdrew by boat to a less vulnerable spot (Matthew 14:13).

The fox, for his part, remained fascinated with this new prophet, following the news of his progress through Galilee and on to Judea and Jerusalem. In this, of course, Herod Antipas was not alone: much of Palestine was watching eagerly to see what would happen when Jesus arrived at the Holy City. As the ruler of Galilee and Perea, Herod Antipas was not directly concerned with Jesus' actions in Jerusalem. However, Luke's Gospel reports that, following his arrest and subsequent questioning by Pontius Pilate, the Roman governor of Judea sent Jesus to Herod Antipas, who was also present in Jerusalem for the Passover feast (Luke 23:6-12). As Jesus was a native of Galilee, Pilate may have reasoned that Herod Antipas had jurisdiction over him. Passing the problem to Herod would also, from Pilate's point of view, have served to free him from a political bind: the temple authorities were calling for Jesus' execution but, during the Passover festival with Jerusalem rammed solid with pilgrims, Pilate evidently had no

wish to inflame an already volatile situation by putting a reputed Jewish prophet to death. For his part, Herod Antipas had evidently heard much of Jesus' reputation as a miracle worker and hoped to see such signs from him. But when Jesus refused to respond to his questions, Herod, affronted, switched to mockery before sending Jesus back to Pilate. He was in Jerusalem: let the Roman governor of the city decide what to do with Jesus. Luke reports that the Roman governor and the Jewish ruler, who had been enemies previously, were reconciled through their common encounter with Jesus.

This is the last mention of Herod Antipas in the Bible. The Herod who imprisons Peter and executes James, son of Zebedee, in the Acts of the Apostles is Herod Agrippa, the grandson of Herod the Great, who was king of Judea from 41 to 44 CE as a result of his friendship with the Emperor Caligula. It was Herod Agrippa who engineered the downfall of his half-uncle by reporting to his childhood friend, Caligula, that Herod Antipas had stockpiled a huge tranche of weapons and was plotting against the emperor. Ever paranoid, Caligula credited Agrippa's story and handed over Herod Antipas' kingdom to Herod Agrippa, sending Herod Antipas into exile in Gaul, most probably in Lugdunum, modern-day Lyon. And there, far from home, Herod Antipas died, sometime after 39 CE.

Death Triumphant

The Romans were masters of pain and they inflicted all their art on rebels and slaves

WRITTEN BY EDOARDO ALBERT

There is one fact that we know more certainly about Jesus than any other: that he died, in agony, hanging on a cross. This is also the second most unusual thing about him: people who died like this were not remembered by history. Crucifixion was a punishment reserved for slaves and rebels, the scum of imperial society. A Roman citizen could not be put to death in such a way. Paul, being a Roman citizen, was beheaded. But Jesus was nailed to a cross.

During its long history, the Roman Empire crucified tens of thousands of people. The Empire imposed peace and order within its borders, but it was a peace built on power, and cemented by terror. In comparison to their Greek subjects, the Romans were a pragmatic people but they were artists in pain. Crucifixion was a punishment designed to humiliate and destroy, to expose the dying to the fact of their own impotence in the face of imperial might, and to remind all those watching—and crucifixion was always a public spectacle—what the power that had consigned the dying man to the cross might do to them. Particular savagery was reserved for rebellious slaves and if a slave should kill his master, then all the slaves of the household—men, women, and children alike—were crucified, regardless of involvement in the murder. Crucifixion was the theater of cruelty as political spectacle. And its aim was to obliterate the memory of the man so killed.

The Romans reserved such punishments to themselves. Only the governor of Judea, Pontius Pilate, might command such a death and so the Sanhedrin brought Jesus to Pilate so that he might be subject to the full spectrum of imperial might. Or that is what the Gospels say and they are the only extant account of Jesus' trial before Pilate, Roman imperial historians not being concerned with the execution of slaves and non-Romans. But how accurate an account do the Gospels give of the deathly proceedings?

Jesus Before Pilate

There is vigorous debate today among scholars as to the historicity of the Gospels' account of Jesus' trial by Pilate, with a significant number of writers arguing that the events, as presented by the evangelists, are not historical but rather the result of the bitter split in the latter part of the first century between the Christian church, composed of Jews who accepted Jesus as the promised Messiah, Gentiles not required to accept the Mosaic law, and Jews who did not accept Jesus as Messiah. According to this view, the role of Pilate in the trial and condemnation of Jesus is downplayed and the blame shifted on to the Jewish people in general and the Jewish authorities in particular. Thus, the main movers in the plot to arrest and try Jesus are the Jewish high priest and his council, while Pilate is presented, in the Gospel accounts, as being somewhat reluctant to hand over for execution a man in whom he can find no guilt. According to this view, the Gospels are essentially theological and sectarian in their accounts of Jesus' trial before Pilate, and their value as a historical record of what actually happened should be discounted. According to this view, they can be read

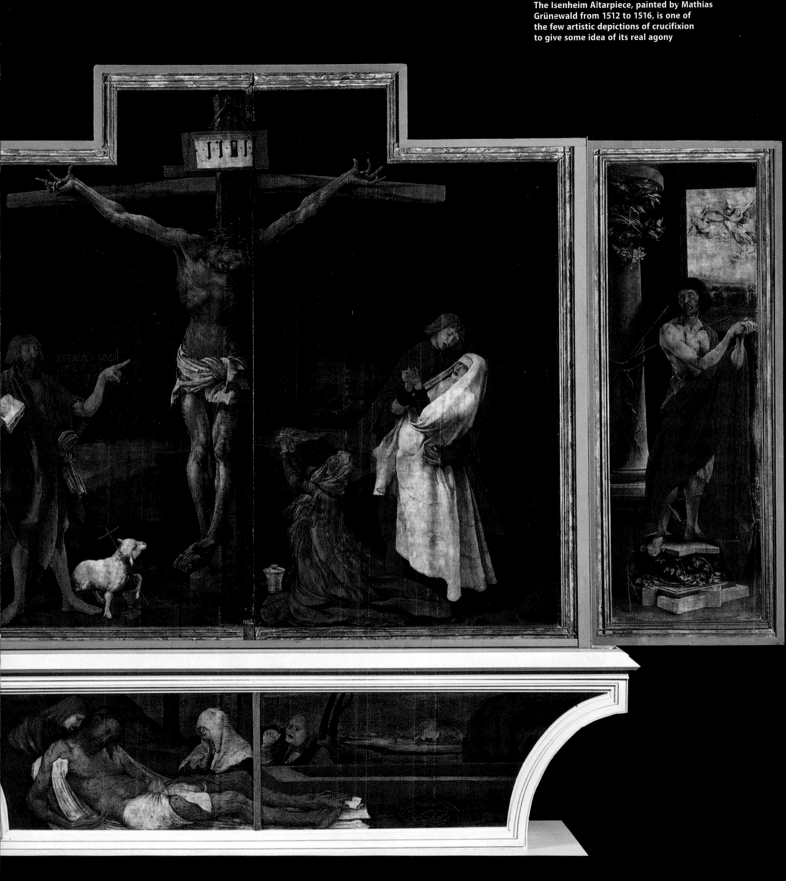

Part of the Via Dolorosa in Jerusalem, the route traditionally held to be the one that Jesus took on the way to his crucifixion

Burial Cloth or Medieval Forgery?

The Turin Shroud is a cloth, kept since 1578 in Turin Cathedral, that has the faint image of a crucified man upon it. Debate continues as to whether it is the burial shroud of Jesus, with no obvious sign of a definite conclusion. The evidence for the shroud being a forgery relies largely upon the carbon-14 dating of the Shroud that took place in 1988, which unambiguously found the sample of cloth it took for testing to date from somewhere between 1260 and 1390. There have been various criticisms of the testing, ranging from the sample tested being mixed with later thread used to repair damage to the Shroud to contamination by layers of bacteria caused by centuries of handling, but these have been discounted by skeptics of the authenticity of the cloth. One point seldom discussed is that, contrary to normal dating methodology, a sample was taken from only one place on the Shroud, rather than from a number of locations. If this had been done, the dating would have been much more reliable. As to the evidence in favor of the Shroud being genuine, perhaps the most obvious is how it shows a man who has been nailed through the wrists. However, the depictions of Jesus crucified from the time period of the carbon dating show Jesus as nailed through the hands. It seems strange that a medieval forger should depart from the common practice in the depiction of Jesus by showing him as nailed through the wrists rather than the hands. ∎

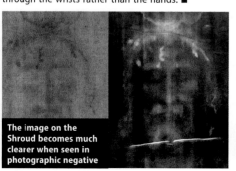

The image on the Shroud becomes much clearer when seen in photographic negative

only in light of the growing discord between the nascent Christian church and a Judaism reeling after the shock of the destruction of the temple in Jerusalem in 70 CE. A corollary of this argument is the late dating of the composition of the Gospels, to the final decades of the 1st century. It is an argument made more urgent by the lamentable history of Christian and secular anti-Semitism in the centuries following the adoption of Christianity as the state religion of the Roman Empire, on through the Middle Ages and Renaissance, up until modern times and the mutation of anti-Semitism into Nazi ideology, resulting in the Holocaust. However, it is also an argument that risks judging the particular, the Gospel accounts of Jesus' trial, through the prism of later events, and as such requires careful evaluation; the dreadful deeds done centuries later should not affect our judgement of texts that preceded these events.

With this in mind, how much credence can we give to what the Gospels say about Jesus' trial before Pilate? The argument for the accounts being completely ahistorical fails on the first count because Pilate, Annas, and Caiaphas, the Jewish religious authorities, are historical figures, attested in records and archaeology. Caiaphas, the high priest, is so historic his very bones have been found in an ossuary discovered in 1990 in Jerusalem. However, the more serious charge is that the account of the trial has been slanted to exonerate Pilate— and by extension, the Roman authorities—

and to place the blame on the Jewish people. Is there any evidence to suggest that the account of what took place in the Gospels is accurate?

There is. Josephus, the Jewish historian, in his book *The Antiquities of the Jews*, tells of a trial by the Sanhedrin, and execution by a reluctant Roman governor. Only this trial took place in 62 CE, the Roman governor was Albinus, and the leader of the Sanhedrin was Ananus ben Ananus, son of Annas and brother-in-law of Caiaphas. And the man on trial was James, "the brother of Jesus who was called the Christ." This account, by a historian with no link to the new Christian cult, parallels the accounts as told in the Gospels and suggests that it was certainly possible for the Jewish authorities to make use of the Roman imperial power to rid themselves of troublemakers.

Furthermore, Josephus shows that the main actors in the condemnation of James were the Temple authorities, as indeed do the Gospels in their account of Jesus' trial, not the wider Jewish population. Indeed, when Jesus is led to Golgotha, the place of execution, the (Jewish) population of Jerusalem followed, weeping at what was about to befall him.

Death by Torture

The accounts of Pilate, in the Gospels and secular histories, agree that he was, above all else, a political fixer: principles or the life of an innocent man made no odds before pleasing his master in Rome. The

> "The accounts of Pilate agree that he was a political fixer: principles or the life of an innocent man made no odds before pleasing his master in Rome"

This graffito, discovered near the Palatine Hill in Rome, may be the earliest depiction of Jesus crucified, dating between the late 1st to the early 3rd centuries

The text reads, "Alexamenos worships [his] God." It is clearly intended to mock Alexamenos and his religion

A Roman scourging could easily kill a man: one reason for Jesus' relatively quick death on the cross may have been the severity of the scourging inflicted upon him

Traditional devotions have Jesus falling three times while carrying the cross. The man on the Turin Shroud appears to have a broken nose, suggesting that he had fallen flat on his face

emperor required from the governor of Judea a quiet and stable province that paid its taxes and did not call upon the legions. To that end, Pilate, in an act of realpolitick that has all too many parallels through the ages, was more than prepared to sacrifice an innocent man to preserve his career and his power. Not that he did not try to wriggle out of the responsibility. First, according to Luke (23:7-15), Pilate tries to offload the problem on to Herod Antipas. Since Jesus was a Galilean, and Herod was the ruler of that province and providentially in town for the Passover, Pilate sent Jesus to him. Herod, having heard of Jesus' reputation as a miracle worker, was keen to see him

perform some party tricks, but when Jesus would not even work one small miracle, Herod subsequently sent him back to Pilate. Herod, a consumate political operator, was not going to be outmaneuvered by another.

Pilate made a final effort to worm out of the responsibility by offering to release Jesus as it was his practice at Passover to pardon a condemned criminal. However, when the hired thugs of the Sadducean priesthood chanted for the release of Barabbas, a notorious bandit, rather than Jesus, Pilate knew that there was no more wiggle room.

Theatrically washing his hands of responsibility, he nevertheless gave the order that Jesus be crucified, for there was

no other authority who could give such an order.

But first Pilate had Jesus whipped. The Gospels pass over this in a word. However, Roman scourging was designed to rip not just the skin but to tear the flesh from a man's back. The whip was multi-thonged, and set with metal. The worst scourges, called scorpions, had hooks. Two soldiers, each armed with a whip, generally alternated strokes, the thongs curling round the body and pulling out strips of flesh.

After such a punishment, it is little surprise that Jesus could not manage to carry the crosspiece of his execution all the way to Golgotha, the "place of the skull," where the upright would have been set, waiting for its load of dying flesh. The soldiers escorting him grabbed a hapless passerby, named Simon of Cyrene (a city in north Africa, near the present-day city of Shahhat in Libya), to carry the crosspiece for Jesus.

There, outside the city walls, the execution squad nailed Jesus' arms to the crossbeam, hammering the nails between the radius and ulna above the wrist rather than through the palm of the hand (a nail through the hand would simply rip through the flesh under the weight of the body). The nail also cut the median nerve, producing the characteriztic crucifixion clench, where the little and ring fingers are fully flexed, the middle finger partially extended and the index finger fully extended (severing the median nerve caused excruciating pain as well, to go with all the other agonies of crucifixion). This hand position has become a gesture of benediction within the Christian church, although historians are not sure whether it derives from Jesus' crucifixion or has another source.

Contrary to the modesty that is accorded to Jesus when he is normally depicted on

The Tomb of Jesus

According to the Gospel accounts, Jesus was buried in a tomb carved into the rock outside the walls of Jerusalem (Jewish law forbidding burial within the city). But the Church of the Holy Sepulchre, which contains the aedicule that is said to mark the site of Jesus' tomb, lies within the city walls. However, historians have shown that the walls were extended after Jesus' death. To repair damage to the aedicule, restorers opened it for 60 hours in 2017. The limestone bed on which Jesus was supposed to have been lain has been covered in marble since at least 1555, but the restorers removed the cladding to examine what was beneath. The church itself has been attacked, suffered earthquakes and been completely rebuilt after it was destroyed in 1009 by the Caliph Al Hakim, whose men attempted to destroy the tomb by fire. Could anything have survived? Hidden beneath the marble cladding was another, older marble slab, marked with a cross, resting on top of a long shelf cut into the limestone. The mortar used to fix the lower marble into place has now been dated to 345 CE, the time when the Emperor Constantine ordered the construction of a church over the reputed site of Jesus' burial. As the first emperor to allow Christian practice within the Roman Empire, Constantine sent men to seek the site of Jesus' burial. They were told it lay beneath a pagan temple that the Emperor Hadrian had ordered built on the site following the Jewish revolt from 132-136 CE. The church historian, Eusebius, recounts how the pagan temple was razed and a rock-cut tomb found beneath, around which the church was built. Despite the vicissitudes of the centuries, it is now clear that the aedicule marks this spot. ∎

The bare limestone exposed when the marble slab protecting it was removed from the aedicule in the Church of the Holy Sepulchre. Was this where Jesus' body was laid after his death?

Depictions of Jesus being nailed to the cross invariably show the nails piercing his hands; in reality, they would have gone through his wrist or forearm

"Crucifixion—from which we derive the word 'excruciating'—was an agonizing death but how long the dying took depended on a number of factors"

a crucifix, in reality the soldiers executing Pilate's sentence would have stripped Jesus completely naked before nailing him to the cross. Humiliation was an intrinsic part of the punishment, and the dying man's clothing would also have been spoils for the hard-working soldiers.

Although the Romans crucified tens of thousands of people, only one victim has been excavated. In 1968, the ossuary of Jehohanan (the son of Hagkol) was found in Jerusalem with an iron nail driven through the heel bone. Jehohanan had probably had his feet nailed individually to the sides of the upright, with his arms being tied over the crossbeam. There he would have hung,

until the slow asphyxiation attendant upon the struggle to breathe killed him.

Nailed to the upright, above Jesus' head, was the justification for execution: the King of the Jews. Pilate executed him on the legal grounds that he was a rebel against the Empire and had set himself against the emperor. Of Jesus' many followers, only the women, and the source of John's Gospel, remained with him: the rest fled or were in hiding. Some of his accusers came out of Jerusalem to mock him. Never ones to miss the opportunity to drive home to the crowd the message that opposing the Empire meant the most dreadful of deaths, the Romans crucified two other men alongside Jesus.

Crucifixion—from which we derive the word "excruciating"—literally "from the cross"—was an agonizing death, but how long the dying took depended on a number of factors, from how the victim was attached to the cross, through his health and age, to how severely he had been whipped before being crucified. Jesus, it would seem, had already been whipped most of the way towards death for he did not last that long on the cross. Some six hours after he was nailed up, he died. It probably didn't feel like a short time to him. The execution squad, to confirm he was dead before allowing the body to be taken down, drove a spear into his chest.

Pilate presented Jesus to the crowd, crying, "Behold the man!" but the hired mob called for the freeing of Barabbas instead

Having received permission from Pilate, Joseph of Arimathea and Nicodemus, two members of the Sanhedrin who were appalled at its decision to seek the execution of Jesus, took the body of Jesus down from the cross, wrapped it in a shroud, and hurriedly laid the corpse to rest in a cave cut into the rock nearby. They had to hurry, for the Sabbath, timed from just before sunset, was drawing near. They laid Jesus in the tomb and sealed the cave with a rock, rolling it into place.

And that was that. Another Messiah dealt with. Another rebel executed. Pilate could go back to the baths, theaters, and gymnasia of Caesarea, where he normally dwelled. The Temple authorities could carry on in charge. It was all over. Death was the great tool of the rich and the powerful and they had wielded it well. Everything was back to normal.

A detail from Pietro Lorenzetti's painting of the Deposition of Christ (taking Jesus down from the cross) in the basilica of St. Francis in Assisi

Artist James Tissot's depiction of what Jesus might have seen from the cross. Note the women disciples in the foreground—the men had run away

© Getty, Wiki

Christ Carrying the Cross

Artist: Anton van Dyck

Year: Early-17th century

In this unconventional scene of Jesus's crucifixion, van Dyck presents an intimate portrait of Christ gazing out to the viewer, dignified and at peace with his fate. Unlike typical scenes of Christ carrying his cross, the crown of thorns is notably absent, while the conspicuous wounds on his hand and the slash on his ribs reflects on the fate of Jesus.

Defeating Death

Crucifixion was the end: the destruction of a person and all that they stood for. But then, something happened . . .

WRITTEN BY EDOARDO ALBERT

Simon bar Giora. Eleazar ben Simon. Lukuas. Simon bar Kokhba. Ever heard of them? These were leaders of the three major Jewish revolts, conflicts that claimed hundreds of thousands, possibly millions, of lives. Apart from historians, few people today know their names. And these were the leaders of the great revolts, the ones that made the history books and that called out the legions. Jesus had, in comparison, a few score followers and of these, all but the women deserted him as he hung dying upon the cross.

He should have been completely forgotten. Swallowed into silence when the last of his followers died. Maybe one or two might have reminisced to their children about the hope that had briefly spluttered in their hearts that this man might be the Messiah who would lead his people to freedom. But then the Temple authorities had arrested him, the Romans had crucified him, and the hope died.

That was what should have happened. That was what happened with all the other prophets and leaders and messiahs who were crushed beneath the grinding wheels of imperial might.

But Jesus wasn't forgotten. Today, Yeshua, the son of a poor carpenter from Nazareth, remains probably the most important person in human history. Indeed, history itself, so often the record of conquerors and killers, of the rich and the powerful, revolves upon the fulcrum of the birth of a man most of the history makers would not even have deigned to speak to, so far below them did Jesus rank socially.

The reason for this is what happened in the 40 or so confusing, disorientating, extraordinary days after Jesus had died, and the reaction of his followers to what they believed they had seen during those days.

On the Third Day

Jesus was probably executed on a Friday, his body was then taken down from the cross and hurriedly buried in a stone tomb just outside the city before the start of the Sabbath at sunset. On the Sabbath, no work was allowed, so the body rested, untended, in the tomb, the blood of crucifixion and scourging crusting the corpse. Then, on Sunday, which was the third day, Jesus' most devoted and bravest followers, the women, traveled early to the tomb in order to wash and anoint the body, to dress Jesus properly for death. That was when they found the tomb empty.

At this point we leave history and enter something much more strange. The accounts in the Gospels of what happened are fragmentary and confusing: the accounts of people who did not know what to make of what was happening post-crucifixion. Jesus' disciples had scattered, taking cover so that they did not get caught up in the aftermath of his death. A couple of them, after the Sabbath was over, decided to head north, back to the relative safety of Galilee. While on the road north out of Jerusalem to Emmaus they fell in with a stranger and started speaking with him about the recent events in the city. Reaching Emmaus, they asked the stranger to stop with them, as the hour was getting late. Sitting at a table, the stranger broke bread with them and, doing

so, the two disciples suddenly recognized him as Jesus, but then he disappeared from their sight.

This is typical of the recorded appearances of Jesus after his death: he is physical and corporeal, breaking bread, cooking fish, eating; he is sometimes recognized and sometimes not; he is able to pass through physical barriers and yet the marks of his death are still apparent on his body. No wonder the people who experienced this found it all but impossible to put into words. But they made no effort to make it make more sense, nor to hide the awkward fact that among the earliest witnesses were women—those unreliable witnesses whose testimony was not acceptable in a court of law at the time.

Paul's letters are generally accepted to be the earliest Christian documents that we have, and he records the appearances that transformed Jesus' followers from a frightened, leaderless rabble into something new: "He appeared to Cephas [Peter], then to the Twelve. Then he appeared to more than five hundred brothers and sisters at one time, most of whom are still alive, though some have died. Then he appeared to James, then to all the Apostles. Last of all, as to one untimely born, he appeared also to me." (Cor. 15:5-8)

Note that Paul, writing to a mixed Gentile and Jewish community under Roman law in the Greek city of Corinth, does not mention the separate appearances to the women.

When coupled with the introduction to this record of Jesus' appearances after his crucifixion—"Christ died for our sins in accordance with the scriptures, and that he

© Heritage Images / Getty

130 STORY OF JESUS

Piero della Francesco's masterpiece is in the Palazzo della Residenza in Sansepolcro, Italy. It shows Jesus stepping from his tomb, the soldiers who had been left to guard the site lying asleep at his feet (Matthew 27:62-66)

The view of Jerusalem from the Mount of Olives. The village of Bethany, on the Mount of Olives, was home to Mary, Martha, and Lazarus, who were particular friends of Jesus

The Ascension

The fullest accounts of the Ascension are in Luke's Gospel and the Acts of the Apostles, written by the same author. According to these versions, Jesus continued to appear to his disciples for 40 days after his Resurrection but then took his disciples to the village of Bethany, where after speaking to them he was taken up into heaven. Bethany is the present-day town of al-Eizariya, lying 1.5 miles east of Jerusalem. It was the home of the siblings Martha, Mary, and Lazarus, particular friends of Jesus. There is a brief description of the Ascension in Mark's Gospel, and allusions to it in the letters and John's Gospel. As an event, it appears to have been as mysterious as any of the post-Crucifixion appearances and while it has been a favorite topic of artists through the centuries, none have really managed to avoid the trap of depicting Jesus riding into the sky on an invisible elevator. As an event, it is probably best understood as the end of the extraordinary period following the Crucifixion when disciples believed that Jesus appeared to them in person. ∎

was buried, and that he was raised on the third day in accordance with the scriptures" (1 Cor 15:3-4)—we have the core belief of the early Christians (although at this point they were not called, even by themselves, Christians, but rather followers of the Way). This is what they went out into the Empire and the world to preach. They were a bunch of fishermen, laborers, tax collectors, and even a tent maker from the fractious corner of the Mediterranean that polite members of society preferred to ignore. They found an initial audience from the lower strata of imperial society: the urban poor, women, and the innumerable slaves whose labor maintained the elaborate structure of the Empire. According to tradition, all but one of the Twelve Paul mentions in his letter to

the Corinthians died in the course of telling this story, and Paul died too. It was quite some story for so many to die for it—and the reason they died for it was because they believed it to be true.

What Sort of Resurrection?

There can be no doubt that the early followers of Jesus believed that he had risen from the dead. But what did that mean at the time and in the written records of what had happened that were written in the subsequent decades? Many scholars have argued that the Gospels were theological documents, presenting a religious argument in a narrative, historical form. As such, the empty tomb and the resurrection appearances of Jesus could not be seen as other than theological events; the response of the early Christian community to the trauma of the death of Jesus and the subsequent experience of his presence, in some sort of mystical and spiritual way. Furthermore, the resurrection appearances were written to cement the claims to leadership in the nascent church of those who could claim to be the key witnesses to Jesus after his death: Peter, John, and Paul. This is resurrection as small-group politics, the sort of struggle for power that you will find in parish councils and social clubs. Only, this was a small church social club that expanded the story it told to itself of its making to take in much of the world.

However, the most interesting contemporary scholarship argues that the Gospels are testaments, the records of direct, named eyewitnesses as to the events of Jesus' life, rather than the products of an oral tradition passed along by many anonymous sources until eventually they were written down. By this view, the early Christian community cared deeply about exactly what Jesus had said and done, and

A local tradition among Christians in Palestine that Jesus ascended from a site on the Mount of Olives by Bethany was recognized after official toleration of the religion and a church built on the site, which was later destroyed by Persian and then Muslim conquerors. There is a chapel on the site today, next to a mosque

A view over Jerusalem from the mid-19th century with the Mount of Olives (site of Jesus' Ascension) rising above the city in the background

Witnessing the Resurrection

Doubting Thomas
(John 20:24-29)

Thomas called the Twin, was one of the Twelve, the body of disciples whose number recapitulated the 12 tribes of Israel. But when Jesus first appeared to the Twelve Thomas was not among them, and he refused to believe in the reality of Jesus' resurrection unless he was able to put his finger through the holes the nails had made in Jesus' hands, and put his hand into the slash in Jesus' side. Eight days later, when Thomas was with the other Apostles, Jesus appeared to them, and holding out his hands, told Thomas to put his finger in the holes, and to put his hand into the gash in Jesus' side. Thomas, seeing Jesus, fell to his knees, saying, "My Lord and my God."

Mary Magdalene
(John 20:11-18)

Mary Magdalene went early on Sunday morning to the tomb to anoint the body, but she found the stone sealing the tomb had been rolled away. She returned with Peter and John, who saw the tomb was empty, and left her there. Mary wept. Then a man, whom she took to be the gardener, asked why she cried, and she asked him if he knew where the body of Jesus was. The man called her by name, "Mary." Hearing her name, Mary knew him, and replied, in Aramaic, "Rabboni," which means teacher. Mary would have clung to him, but Jesus told her to go and tell the disciples that he would ascend to his father. And that is what she did.

The Empty Tomb
(Mark 16:1-7)

The women were the first to go to minister to Jesus' dead body: Mary Magdalene, Jesus' mother, and Salome. They went carrying spices to anoint the body, and probably water and cloths to wash the blood from the corpse that had been so hurriedly buried, although they wondered who they could ask to roll away the cap stone so they could do their job. But reaching the tomb, they found the stone rolled away, and inside the tomb a man in white, who, pointing to the empty slab where Jesus' body had been lain, told them that he was risen. "Go, tell his disciples and Peter that he is going before you to Galilee. There you will see him, just as he told you."

specific eyewitnesses (including the Twelve but not limited to them) told their stories of what Jesus had said and done, and these stories were valued precisely because they were told by eyewitnesses who could vouch for their veracity. This was the model of the first Christian communities, which only began to change a few decades later, when these eyewitnesses began to die off. The Gospels were written then to preserve this eyewitness testimony and, to indicate this same sentiment to future readers. They were framed in this way as they were being written in accordance with the best sort of history of the time, which valued the evidence of people who had participated in the recorded events more highly than anything else.

Of course, whether the evidence of these witnesses is credible is another matter entirely, and one that has much more to do with the readers' view of the possibility or otherwise of events outside and contrary to everyday occurrences. In Matthew's Gospel, Jesus asks his followers what the talk is on the street and in the towns about him, and they tell Jesus that some people say that he is a prophet, and others say that he is Elijah, or Jeremiah, or John the Baptist. "But you," asks Jesus, "who do you say I am?" Today, two thousand years later, the question still leaps off the page with the same urgency, the same importance as when it was first posed by Jesus.

"But you, who do you say I am?"

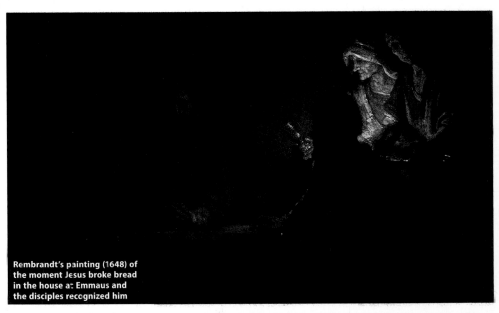

Rembrandt's painting (1648) of the moment Jesus broke bread in the house at Emmaus and the disciples recognized him

According to tradition, Ascension Rock within the Chapel of the Ascension was where Jesus stood before being taken up into heaven

The Ascension of Christ
Artist: Il Perugino
Year: 1495-98

Commissioned to create a 15-piece altarpiece for a Benedictine monastery, the only remaining elements depict the Ascension of Christ. Like other artworks of the same scene, the canvas is split into two halves—the Earthly ascension, and the Heavenly ascension. In this painting, Christ rises above the 12 Apostles and Saint Paul, as well as the Virgin Mary, who stands directly beneath him. In a surviving lunette painting that stands above this scene, God looks down from Heaven to his ascending son.

EARLY CHRISTIANITY

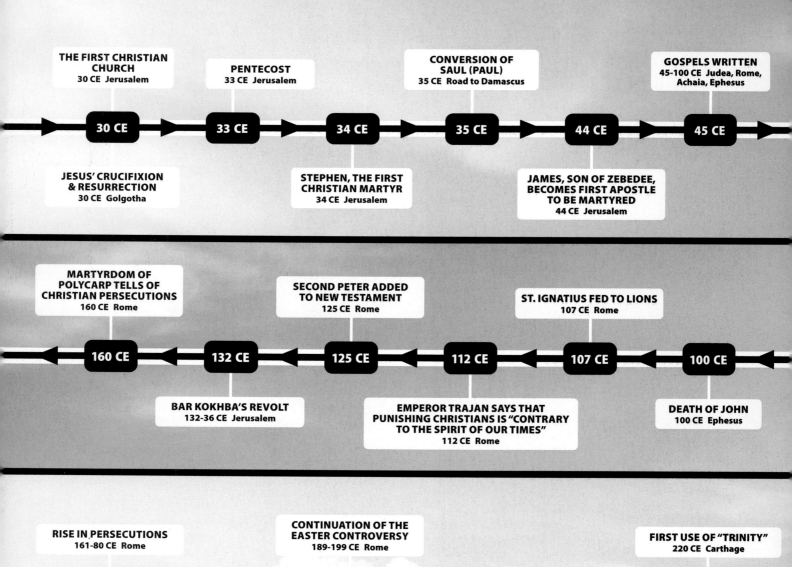

THE FIRST CHRISTIAN CHURCH
30 CE Jerusalem

PENTECOST
33 CE Jerusalem

CONVERSION OF SAUL (PAUL)
35 CE Road to Damascus

GOSPELS WRITTEN
45-100 CE Judea, Rome, Achaia, Ephesus

30 CE → 33 CE → 34 CE → 35 CE → 44 CE → 45 CE

JESUS' CRUCIFIXION & RESURRECTION
30 CE Golgotha

STEPHEN, THE FIRST CHRISTIAN MARTYR
34 CE Jerusalem

JAMES, SON OF ZEBEDEE, BECOMES FIRST APOSTLE TO BE MARTYRED
44 CE Jerusalem

MARTYRDOM OF POLYCARP TELLS OF CHRISTIAN PERSECUTIONS
160 CE Rome

SECOND PETER ADDED TO NEW TESTAMENT
125 CE Rome

ST. IGNATIUS FED TO LIONS
107 CE Rome

160 CE ← 132 CE ← 125 CE ← 112 CE ← 107 CE ← 100 CE

BAR KOKHBA'S REVOLT
132-36 CE Jerusalem

EMPEROR TRAJAN SAYS THAT PUNISHING CHRISTIANS IS "CONTRARY TO THE SPIRIT OF OUR TIMES"
112 CE Rome

DEATH OF JOHN
100 CE Ephesus

RISE IN PERSECUTIONS
161-80 CE Rome

CONTINUATION OF THE EASTER CONTROVERSY
189-199 CE Rome

FIRST USE OF "TRINITY"
220 CE Carthage

161 CE → 185 CE → 189 CE → 200 CE → 203 CE → 220 CE

SAINT APOLLONIUS USES TERM "CATHOLIC"
185 CE Alexandria

SEXTUS JULIUS AFRICANUS CALCULATES TIME BETWEEN CREATION AND JESUS AS 5,500 YEARS
200 CE Emmaus

MARTYRDOM OF PERPETUA, A YOUNG WOMAN WHO WROTE A JOURNAL OF HER TRIAL AND IMPRISONMENT
203 CE Carthage

Timeline of Key Events

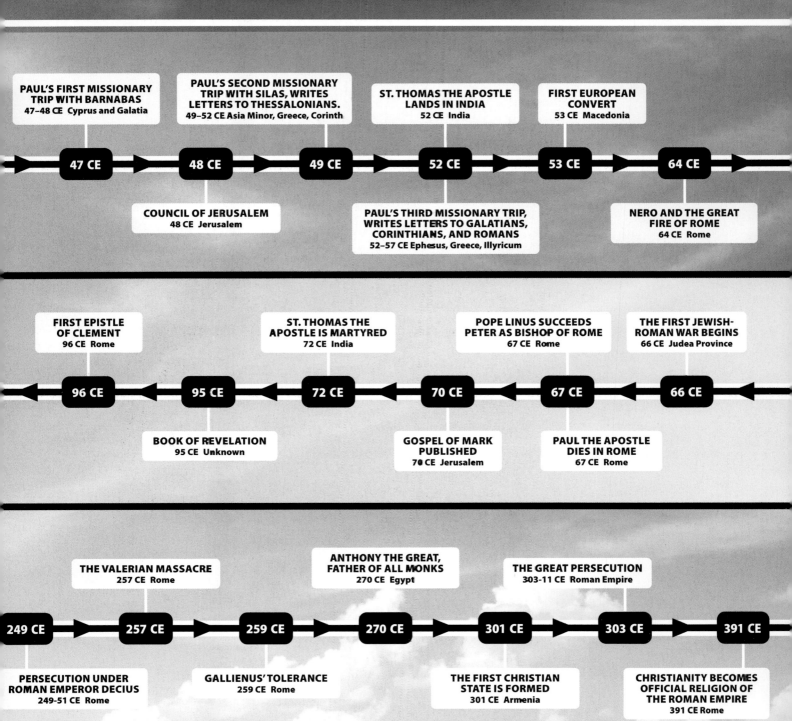

PAUL'S FIRST MISSIONARY TRIP WITH BARNABAS
47–48 CE Cyprus and Galatia

PAUL'S SECOND MISSIONARY TRIP WITH SILAS, WRITES LETTERS TO THESSALONIANS.
49–52 CE Asia Minor, Greece, Corinth

ST. THOMAS THE APOSTLE LANDS IN INDIA
52 CE India

FIRST EUROPEAN CONVERT
53 CE Macedonia

47 CE → 48 CE → 49 CE → 52 CE → 53 CE → 64 CE →

COUNCIL OF JERUSALEM
48 CE Jerusalem

PAUL'S THIRD MISSIONARY TRIP, WRITES LETTERS TO GALATIANS, CORINTHIANS, AND ROMANS
52–57 CE Ephesus, Greece, Illyricum

NERO AND THE GREAT FIRE OF ROME
64 CE Rome

FIRST EPISTLE OF CLEMENT
96 CE Rome

ST. THOMAS THE APOSTLE IS MARTYRED
72 CE India

POPE LINUS SUCCEEDS PETER AS BISHOP OF ROME
67 CE Rome

THE FIRST JEWISH-ROMAN WAR BEGINS
66 CE Judea Province

← 96 CE ← 95 CE ← 72 CE ← 70 CE ← 67 CE ← 66 CE ←

BOOK OF REVELATION
95 CE Unknown

GOSPEL OF MARK PUBLISHED
70 CE Jerusalem

PAUL THE APOSTLE DIES IN ROME
67 CE Rome

THE VALERIAN MASSACRE
257 CE Rome

ANTHONY THE GREAT, FATHER OF ALL MONKS
270 CE Egypt

THE GREAT PERSECUTION
303-11 CE Roman Empire

249 CE → 257 CE → 259 CE → 270 CE → 301 CE → 303 CE → 391 CE

PERSECUTION UNDER ROMAN EMPEROR DECIUS
249-51 CE Rome

GALLIENUS' TOLERANCE
259 CE Rome

THE FIRST CHRISTIAN STATE IS FORMED
301 CE Armenia

CHRISTIANITY BECOMES OFFICIAL RELIGION OF THE ROMAN EMPIRE
391 CE Rome

Events in Early Christianity 30CE–33CE

TITLE	PARAGRAPH
JESUS' CRUCIFIXION AND RESURRECTION **Golgotha • 30 CE** **Matthew 26–28** **Mark 11, 14–16** **Luke 19, 22–24** **John 11–13, 18–20**	During his life, Jesus came to be viewed as a threat both by the Roman authorities and the Jewish council. It led to him being brought before the Roman prefect of Judea, Pontius Pilate, charged with claiming to be the King of the Jews, something which, according to Luke 23:3, he did not deny. Pilate ordered Jesus to be whipped and crucified, a harsh and shameful punishment often reserved for those those seeking to challenge Roman rule or social order. But while Jesus was said to have died within six hours before being placed in a tomb, his followers believe that God raised him from the dead on the third day. After spending forty days appearing to numerous people. Christians say he ascended into heaven. This became known as the Ressurection.
THE FIRST CHRISTIAN CHURCH **Jerusalem • 30 CE** **Matthew 28:16–20**	Shortly before his crucifixion, Jesus had chosen his closest followers—the Twelve Apostles. Christians believe he instructed these dozen men to spread his teaching across the world in an act that has become known as the Great Commission, shortly after the resurrection.

| **PENTECOST**

Jerusalem • 33 CE

Acts 2 | As the Twelve Apostles and 120 other followers of Christ were celebrating the Jewish holiday of the Feast of Weeks, they were visited by the Holy Spirit, who baptized the believers into Christ. This day became known as Pentecost. According to the Book of Acts, Jerusalem then became the first center of the Church, and it is where the Apostles are understood to have lived and taught for a time. |

Events in Early Christianity 34 CE–64 CE

TITLE	PARAGRAPH
STEPHEN, THE FIRST CHRISTIAN MARTYR Jerusalem • 34 CE Acts 6–7	Saint Stephen became one of the first deacons of the Christian Church. His job was to distribute charitable aid to poorer members of the community, but he was also a skilled orator and he effectively spread the word of Christ. Such teachings, however, led him into a conflict with a Jewish synagogue and he was accused of blasphemy. Put on trial at the Sanhedrin, he spoke at length of Israel's idolatry and disobedience. Duly angered, the crowd then dragged him on to the streets and stoned him to death. Paul held the coats of the people who were stoning Stephen.
CONVERSION OF SAUL (PAUL) Road to Damascus 35 CE Acts 9:1–31	Paul never met Jesus and he was not one of the Twelve Apostles, but he did know and talk to many of them. After a dramatic conversion on the road to Damascus, he became one of Christianity's most important figures. His key achievements included teaching the Gospel of Christ far and wide and founding several churches in Europe and Asia. He also wrote thirteen of the twenty-seven books in the New Testament, and he was discussed in great depth in the Acts of the Apostles, which tells of Christianity's spreading message in the Roman Empire.
GOSPELS WRITTEN Judea, Rome, Achaia, Ephesus • 45 CE–100 CE	Matthew, Mark, Luke, and John each wrote their own gripping story of who Jesus was, what he did, and his impact on the people around him. Mark's account is short and fast-moving, Matthew provides a stately and commanding version of Jesus, Luke paints a picture of grand adventure, and John's Gospel is written more elaborately and presents more opportunity for discussion.
COUNCIL OF JERUSALEM Jerusalem • 48 CE Romans 2:12–29	Christianity began to differentiate from Judaism around a quarter of a century after Jesus' death. At that time, a meeting was held to discuss whether non-Jewish (Gentile) men converting from Paganism to Christianity would need to be circumcised. The issue was raised because Jewish law states the practice is an obligatory commandment. However, Hellenistic culture, from which many converts were being drawn, considered it repulsive. After much debate, the Council of Jerusalem reached a compromise: Gentiles did not have to be circumcised but ethnic Jewish Christians were advised to be. This meant the latter could continue to observe the Law of Moses while Gentiles could convert without issue.
FIRST EUROPEAN CONVERT Macedonia • 53 CE Acts 16:11–15	Lydia of Thyatira was a Greek woman who had moved to a Roman settlement in Macedonia called Philippi, where she is said to have sold expensive, purple-dyed cloth. While there she came across the Apostle Paul during his second of three mission journeys and, having heard and believed Paul's proclamation of the Gospel of Christ, Lydia and her household were baptized. She then asked Paul and his party—made up of Silas and Timothy—to stay at her home.
NERO AND THE GREAT FIRE OF ROME Rome • 64 CE	The Great Fire of Rome was a watershed moment for early Christians. Although Emperor Nero has long been blamed for the blaze, the finger was in fact firmly pointed at followers of Jesus at the time. This led to the Roman Empire's first persecution against the Christians. Hundreds were arrested, tortured, and killed. In an arena, Nero had the Christians dressed in animal pelts and torn to pieces by lions. Around the Arena, he had the Christians hung up on crosses and set aflame.

Events in Early Christianity 67 CE–96 CE

TITLE	PARAGRAPH
PAUL THE APOSTLE DIES IN ROME **Rome • 67 CE**	Without Paul, Christianity may never have grown beyond being a small sect of Judaism. But his journeys around the Mediterranean weren't without incident. He was held prisoner in Caesarea Maritima for two years around 58 CE, shipwrecked on Malta, and placed under house arrest in Rome. Some say that he was executed on the orders of the brutal Roman emperor Nero. Around the same time, in 64 CE, the apostle Paul–leader of the disciples–was martyred in Rome by being crucified upside down.
GOSPEL OF MARK PUBLISHED **Jerusalem • 70 CE**	The second book of the New Testament was the first Gospel to be written. As with the other three, the Gospel According to Mark was a selective account of Jesus' life and it told of his baptism by John the Baptist and of his eventual death and burial. The Gospel announces Jesus as the Son of God and word of his teachings and parables.
BOOK OF REVELATION **Unknown • 95 CE**	By the end of the century, other Gospels had been written by Matthew, Luke, and John, but one book that has attracted a lot of subsequent interest is the Book of Revelation. It is said to have been written by the apostle John—who wrote the fourth Gospel—but that has long been disputed. Whoever the author is, the document is entirely apocalyptic, depicting suffering and disaster through a series of visions that include reference to the Whore of Babylon, the Battle of Armageddon, the Horsemen of the Apocalypse, and the seven-headed beast—numbered 666. It has come to be seen as a way of encouraging Christians to be uncompromising with Rome, which had persecuted followers of the religion under Emperor Nero.

FIRST EPISTLE OF CLEMENT **Rome • 96 CE**	Not all Christian documents were included in the canon of the New Testament. Many others would form part of a collection known as the Apostolic Fathers, which included writings from Christian theologians such as Ignatius of Antioch, Clement of Rome, Polycarp of Smyrna, Didache, and Shepherd of Hermas. They represented a generation that had been in contact with the Twelve Apostles, and they were very popular. The First Epistle of Clement was a letter addressed to the Christians in the city of Corinth, and it is understood to be the earliest example of such documents. The letter mainly expressed concern that the Corinthian Church was deposing older men from the ministry. Quoting extensively from the Old Testament, it called for peace and reconciliation. It urged people to look to Jesus and the apostles as examples.

Events in Early Christianity 100 CE–136 CE

TITLE	PARAGRAPH
DEATH OF JOHN Ephesus • 100 CE	John was one of the Twelve Apostles of Jesus and was the only disciple to die of natural causes–the rest were martyred. John lived to be 88 years old, dying of old age peacefully.
ST. IGNATIUS FED TO LIONS Rome • 107 CE	Ignatius of Antioch had converted to Christianity at a young age, and he later became a Bishop of Antioch as well as a keen writer. He wrote six letters en route to Rome after being arrested by the Romans, which addressed the sacraments, ecclesiology, the rejection of a Saturday Sabbath in favor of a Lords Day Sunday, and the role of bishops. He was the first person to use the term "Catholic church" in writing. Ignatius also wrote of his impending death and, indeed, he was taken to the Colosseum and thrown to two lions that devoured him.
SECOND PETER ADDED TO NEW TESTAMENT Rome • 125 CE	The Apostle Peter—who was already known for having appointed Matthias to replace Judas and for allowing Gentiles to join the Church without the need to convert to Judaism first—is understood to have written two epistles, both of which are part of the canon of the New Testament. The first was addressed to people living in the Roman provinces of Asia Minor and it talks of the tests facing Christians. The second—written shortly before his death sixty or so years earlier and accepted into the canon after a period of difficulty–explains that God had delayed the Second Coming of Christ in order that people will be able to lead holy lives, reject evil, and find salvation. In warning them about false teachers, it urged them to grow in their knowledge of Christ.
BAR KOKHBA'S REVOLT Jerusalem • 132-36 CE	The Jews revolted against the Roman Empire in Judaea during the First Jewish-Roman War of 66–73 CE. It led to the Romans being expelled from Jerusalem, only for the rebellion to be later crushed on the orders of Emperor Nero. A second conflict—the Kitos War—was also fought, albeit outside the Judaea Province. A third war later erupted that came to be known as the Bar Kokhba Revolt. Sparked by Emperor Hadrian, who wanted to found a colony on the site of Jerusalem, and by religious and political tension, the Messianic figure Bar Kokhba hoped to drive their enemy away. But the Romans were too strong for them; more than 580,000 Jews died, and many others were sold into slavery. Large Judean communities were dispersed and Jews—along with the Jewish Christians—were banned from entering Jerusalem as harsh new regulations were quickly implemented as punishment.

Events in Early Christianity 161 CE–220 CE

TITLE	PARAGRAPH
RISE IN PERSECUTIONS **Rome • 161-80 CE**	Christianity was well established by this point, and it was spreading rapidly, but not always in its previously accepted form. Departures tended to be labeled as heresy by the Orthodox Church, and that was certainly the case with Gnosticism. Valentinus was a gnostic religious philosopher from Egypt who believed in rival deities of good and evil. But while Christianity was worried about such departures, it also had to deal with continuing persecution. Marcus Aurelius was the Emperor of Rome for nineteen years and persecution of Christians increased during his reign. Whether or not he ordered such treatment or whether he even knew about it has split historians, but those killed included Saint Justin Martyr, who had sought to convert pagans but who had been denounced as subversive, and Polycarp, a Christian bishop of Smyrma who was arrested, bound, and burned in 167 CE.
CONTINUATION OF THE EASTER CONTROVERSY **Rome • 189-199 CE**	In 189 CE, Victor I became the first Bishop of Rome to be born in the Roman Province of Africa. He not only made Latin the official language of the Roman church, but he also waded into the Easter Controversy, which attempted to set a correct date for Easter. Christians in Asia Minor celebrated the day of the Crucifixion on the day Jews celebrated Passover, and the Resurrection was marked two days later. Christians in the West, however, celebrated the Resurrection on the first Sunday after the 14th day of the Jewish month of Nisan. Victor I favored the latter but it was never truly resolved.
EMERGENCE OF THE ANTIPOPE **Rome • 200 CE**	Debate has long raged over who was the first antipope, a title referring to the men who opposed the legitimately elected Bishop of Rome. The Greek historian of Christianity, Eusebius, makes mention of Natalius (c. 200 CE), although Hippolytus of Rome (born in 170 CE and died in 235 CE) is more widely recognized. He came into conflict with Pope Callistus, who was elected in 217 CE, claiming that Callistus held the office of pope even though he didn't have the authority to do so. Hippolytus also reigned in opposition to Callistus' successors Urban I and Pontian, but he did later reconcile with Pontian. That happened when the pair suffered during Roman Emperor Maximinus' persecution of Christians in 235 CE. Exiled together to the mines of Sardinia, they agreed to allow Anterus to succeed them both. They then died as martyrs.
FIRST USE OF "TRINITY" **Carthage • 220 CE**	The Christian author Tertullian was notable for a number of reasons. Writing at a time of persecution, he produced a large body of work in Latin for as many as twenty-five years, which not only earned him the title of "The Father of Latin Christianity" but also helped the religion's spread among western Christians who could understand his work. He was the first writer in Latin to use the term "trinity," and his view was that a single God fulfilled the role of Father, Son, and Holy Spirit. It caused controversy among early Christians who couldn't get their heads around the idea.

Events in Early Christianity 257 CE–270 CE

TITLE	PARAGRAPH
THE VALERIAN MASSACRE Rome • 257 CE	Valerian the Elder was Roman Emperor from 253– 60 CE, but his reign was marked by civil strife and a battle against the Persians. As he tried to keep the empire together, he looked for a scapegoat to deflect attention from his troubles, pointing the finger squarely at the Christians and ordering the Senate—in two letters—to take steps against them. Christians were initially forced to perform sacrifices to the Roman gods, but the persecution escalated in 258 CE when it was ordered that Christian leaders were to be executed. Among those martyred for refusing to worship Roman gods were Pope Sixtus II and seven deacons. Valerian himself was captured by the Persians in 260 CE and imprisoned for life.
GALLIENUS' TOLERANCE Rome • 259 CE	Gallienus had ruled as Roman Emperor with his father, Valerian, then ruled alone from 260–68 CE. He'd made his mark in 259 CE by issuing what was the first official declaration of tolerance regarding the Christians by the Roman Empire. This was a crucial moment for the religion, for while it stopped short of making Christianity an official religion, it did allow places of worship and cemeteries to be restored. The Romans were in effect guaranteeing a right of possession. Christians were also able to appoint their own officers and deal with their dead in the way they saw fit.
ANTHONY THE GREAT, FATHER OF ALL MONKS Egypt • 270 CE	Those who follow a monastic life renounce worldly pursuits and instead devote their lives to spiritual work. This way of life developed early within the Church's history thanks to Anthony the Great, who lived a hermitic life for fifteen years from around the age of eighteen in c. 270 CE, later going on to organize a group of his own disciples into a worshipful community. Inspired, this sparked a surge in the number of similarly withdrawn, monastic groups across Egypt, and Anthony—who had often been referred to as the first Christian monk—came to be known as the "Father of All Monks." The Monastery of Saint Anthony was built between 298 and 300 CE and it stands in an oasis in the eastern desert of Egypt. It is the oldest monastery in the world.

Events in Early Christianity 301 CE–391 CE

TITLE	PARAGRAPH
THE FIRST CHRISTIAN STATE IS FORMED **Armenia • 301 CE**	There is a debate over whether Gregory the Illuminator existed. If he did, and the legend is indeed correct, then he not only managed to introduce Christianity to Armenia, but he also persuaded King Tridates III to make it the country's state religion. The story goes that Gregory's father, Anag, had assassinated King Khosrov II, prompting Gregory to go on the run. When he returned, Tiridates III (son of the murdered king) imprisoned him and tried in vain to get Gregory to renounce Christianity, only to be converted himself. But that matters less than the one fact: Armenia did become the first country in the world to adopt Christianity as its official religion in 301 CE. What's more, the Armenian Apostolic Church is the world's oldest national church.
THE GREAT PERSECUTION **Roman Empire 303-11 CE**	In 303 CE, Christians faced their toughest test yet as the Roman Empire sanctioned a level of persecution more severe than any before it. Acting on a desire to rid the empire of different religions, the Emperors Diocletian, Maximian, Galerius, and Constantius took away the legal rights of Christians and forced them to sacrifice to Roman gods. This subsequently led to the newly built Christian church at Nicomedia being demolished and stripped of its treasures. Followers of the religion were also banned from coming together in worship. Places of worship, books, and scriptures were destroyed, and many Christians were executed. Every bishop, priest, and deacon was also arrested and imprisoned, with scores of Christians burned alive, particularly in the harsher east. Although some sought to save themselves, leading to different church factions emerging, the pain was only truly eased when the Edict of Milan was agreed. This saw Christians treated benevolently across the empire.

TITLE	PARAGRAPH
COUNCIL OF NICAEA **Nicaea • 325 CE**	The Council of Nicaea was the first council in the history of the Christian church that was intended to address all believers. The Nicene creed was written, and the council addressed matters of doctrine.
CHRISTIANITY'S NEW ROLE **Rome • 391 CE**	In 380 CE Emperor Theodosius issued the Edict of Thessalonica, which solidified Christianity as the state religion of the Roman Empire. By 391 CE, the public worship of any other gods was made illegal.